HBO ORIGINAL
THE WHITE LOTUS

OFFICIAL COOKBOOK

HBO ORIGINAL
THE WHITE LOTUS

OFFICIAL COOKBOOK

SIGNATURE RECIPES FROM OUR RESORTS' MOST
POPULAR DESTINATIONS

By Jarrett Melendez

SAN RAFAEL · LOS ANGELES · LONDON

Contents

Introduction 9

CHAPTER ONE
Maui

MORNING SERVICE

Tropical Sunrise Smoothie 12
Loco Moco 15
Coconut French Toast 16
Ricotta Soufflé Pancakes 17
Malasadas 18
Spam Musubi 21
Lomi Lomi Salmon 22
Manapua 25
Garlic Shrimp 28
Poke Bowl 31

EVENING SERVICE

Coconut Seafood Chowder 32
Huli Huli Chicken 35
Seared Sesame-Crusted Mahi Mahi 36
Macadamia-Crusted Pork 37
Fish Tacos 38
Saimin 41
Seared Steak with Shiitake Mushrooms and Miso Butter 42
Macadamia Haupia Tart 45
Coconut Cake 46
Ube-Marbled Butter Mochi 49

CHAPTER TWO

Sicily

MORNING SERVICE

Brioche col Tuppo	52
Coffee Granita	55
Blood Orange and Fennel Salad	56
Warm Ricotta with Lemon and Olive Oil	59
Bruschetta	61
Caponata	62
Sfincione	65
Arancini	66

EVENING SERVICE

Pasta Pescatore	69
Panelle	70
Pasta con Pesto alla Trapanese	73
Pasta alla Norma	74
Pasta con le Sarde	76
Braciole Messinesi	79
Pasta di Mandorla Cookies	80
Cannoli	83
Gelato di Pistacchio	84
Lemon Prosecco Granita	87
Pignolata	88
Cassata	91

CHAPTER THREE

Thailand

MORNING SERVICE

Rice Soup (Khao Tom Goong)	94
Rice Porridge (Jok)	96
Thai-Style Omelet (Khao Khai Chiao)	97
Roti	99
Sour Curry (Kaeng Som)	100
Tom Yum Goong	103
Massaman Curry (Kaeng Massaman)	104
Satay	107
Nam Prik Goong Siap	108

EVENING SERVICE

Yellow Curry (Kaeng Kari)	109
Chicken Biryani (Khao Mok Gai)	110
Lime Pork (Moo Manao)	113
Pad Thai Goong	114
Tom Kha Gai	117
"Rainbow" Rice Salad (Khao Yum)	118
Crab Fried Rice (Khao Phat Poo)	121
Crispy Pork (Moo Krop)	122
Thai Iced Tea	125
Banana Pancakes (Roti Pisang)	126
Sticky Rice and Mango	129

Dietary Considerations	130
Measurement Conversions	133
About the Author	135
Acknowledgments	135
Index	139

Aloha, buongiorno, and สวัสดี!

From all of us at The White Lotus, we thank you for choosing to let us be a part of your vacation. Now, we're thrilled to join you in your own kitchen with this cookbook. As with any feature of our resorts, our goal is your satisfaction. Why? Well, because you deserve it, of course. Just because you're not currently at a White Lotus resort doesn't mean you don't deserve to take a moment for yourself, get in the kitchen (or have your personal chef do it for you), and taste a little bit of paradise amid the hustle and bustle of your everyday life.

In this book, you'll find tantalizing local delicacies from three of our popular destinations: Maui, Sicily, and Southern Thailand. Any one of them will bring you right back to your favorite White Lotus resort. With favorite dishes selected from both our morning and evening service menus, this curated collection will ensure each moment of your day is an *experience*.

Longing to return to the golden sunrises and endless oceans of the magnificent coastlines of our Maui location? Then perhaps you could start your morning with pillowy Malasadas (page 18). For dinner, share a few bowls of savory Saimin (page 41) as you end your day among friends and family, and finish the evening with a creamy slice of Macadamia Haupia Tart (page 45). Its crunchy, golden crust laden with buttery macadamia nuts is proof positive that "good things happen to good people," as one of our *notable* guests once said.

Or perhaps you'd rather return to the deep blue seas of Sicily, where you can start your day with warm, buttery Brioche col Tuppo (page 52) and a glistening goblet of Coffee Granita (page 55). Then finish your evening with sumptuous Pasta alla Norma (page 74) and a bowl of decadent Gelato di Pistacchio (page 84). It's enough to make you forget the discourse, at least for a moment.

If the cuisine of Southern Thailand calls to you, start re-creating our hearty Rice Soup (page 94), then try your hand at the national dish of Thailand, Pad Thai Goong (page 114). You might finish your day with the dreamy, crowd-pleasing Sticky Rice and Mango (page 129).

There's no right or wrong way to enjoy cooking through this book, just like there's no wrong way to enjoy your stay at a White Lotus resort. If you want to mix and match cuisines to eat your way around the world in a day, who's to stop you from having Thai for breakfast, Hawaiian for lunch, and Sicilian for dinner? Not a single person, that's who. Throw in a spa treatment while you're at it.

Until your next visit, we hope this cookbook gives you a taste of your home away from home.

Sincerely,
Your Friends at The White Lotus Resort & Spa

CHAPTER ONE
Maui

Perhaps you've stayed at our tropical paradise in Maui and wish to relive some of those magical meals on the terrace of your suite, during a luau, or on an intimate boat tour arranged by a member of our staff. If you've yet to visit our Maui location, surely it's on your bucket list. But you may want a sampling of the pleasures and delights that await you on our exquisite island property—what better way to entice you to pay us a visit? Throughout this chapter, you'll find recipes for dishes that both celebrate and elevate Hawaiian seafood, meats, and produce, from ubiquitous local staples like Spam Musubi (page 21) and Loco Moco (page 15) to signature White Lotus dishes served in our fine dining rooms, like Coconut Seafood Chowder (page 32) and Seared Sesame-Crusted Mahi Mahi (page 36). One sip, bite, or spoonful will transport you right here with us, where we await your arrival with leis, welcome cocktails, and big smiles. Aloha!

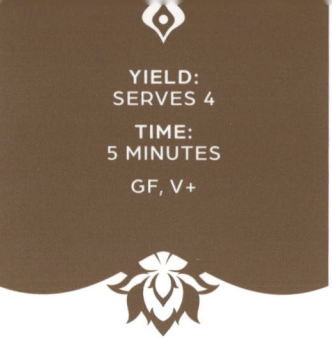

YIELD:
SERVES 4

TIME:
5 MINUTES

GF, V+

- 2 tablespoons chia seeds
- ¼ cup plant-based vanilla protein powder
- 1 large banana, sliced
- 1½ cups frozen pineapple chunks
- ½ cup frozen mango chunks
- 1 cup frozen strawberries
- 1 tablespoon fresh lime juice
- 2 cups coconut milk

Special Equipment
Blender

MORNING SERVICE

Tropical Sunrise Smoothie

Whether you rise with the sun or decide to sleep in, perhaps after a night exploring all the island has to offer, our breakfast buffet awaits (included for all of our Blossom Circle members). Break your fast with one of our signature tropical blends from the smoothie bar, featuring a dazzling array of local produce, harvested mere yards from the property. Whip up one of these smoothies at home and you'll swear you can hear the waves crashing on the beach below your windows.

Add the ingredients in the order listed to the carafe of a blender. Blend on low speed, then gradually increase the speed to high. Blend until smooth and creamy, 2 to 3 minutes.

Divide the smoothie among four glasses and serve.

YIELD:
SERVES 4

TIME:
1 HOUR

Beef Patties
1 pound lean ground beef
1 large egg
¼ cup panko
2 cloves garlic, grated
2 scallions, minced (white and light green parts only)
2 teaspoons Worcestershire sauce
1 teaspoon soy sauce
¼ teaspoon kosher salt
½ teaspoon black pepper
1 tablespoon extra virgin olive oil

Gravy
2 tablespoons cornstarch
1 tablespoon water
2 teaspoons soy sauce
1 teaspoon rice vinegar
1 medium sweet onion, sliced
8 ounces shiitake mushroom caps, cleaned and sliced
2 cups beef stock

For Assembly
4 cups steamed short- or medium-grain white rice
4 sunny-side-up eggs

Loco Moco

Start your day off right with a heaping bowl of Hawaiian comfort food. For guests who may have enjoyed a few too many the night before (don't worry, we'll never tell), this savory go-to has been touted as an excellent hangover cure. The most traditional preparation of this dish starts with a bed of rice, a well-seared beef patty, gravy, and a sunny-side-up egg. We've kept close to tradition with this version, adding some shiitake mushrooms to the gravy. The egg on top is key—just picture it smiling up at you as the sun's rays beam down.

To make the beef patties: Crumble the ground beef into a large bowl. Add the egg, panko, garlic, scallions, Worcestershire sauce, soy sauce, salt, and pepper. Mix well with your hands to a uniform texture. Divide into 4 equal patties, flattening each to about ¼ inch thick. Transfer to a platter and chill, uncovered, for 20 minutes. (To chill more than 20 minutes, wrap with foil or plastic wrap.)

While the patties chill, make the slurry for the gravy. In a small bowl, whisk together the cornstarch, water, soy sauce, and rice vinegar until smooth. Set aside.

Once the patties are chilled, heat the olive oil in a large skillet over medium-high heat until shimmering, about 2 minutes. Add the patties and sear for 1 minute, then decrease the heat to medium. Cook until well seared, about 3 minutes more, then flip. Cook for 3 to 5 minutes more, or until cooked through. Transfer to a plate.

To make the gravy: Drain off excess fat from the patties, leaving 1 to 2 tablespoons in the skillet. Return the skillet to medium-high heat and add the onions and mushrooms. Cook, stirring occasionally, until the onions are translucent and beginning to turn brown, 10 to 15 minutes.

Add the beef stock and use a wooden spoon to scrape up any browned bits that are stuck to the skillet. Bring to a boil and cook until reduced slightly, 3 to 5 minutes. Whisk the cornstarch slurry until smooth, then stir it into the skillet.

Let the mixture boil until thickened, about 3 minutes. Stir frequently. Decrease the heat to a simmer, then add the patties. Cover and cook until just warmed through, 2 to 3 minutes.

To assemble: Divide the rice among four wide, shallow bowls. Place a patty on top of each mound of rice, and top with 2 to 3 spoonfuls of the gravy. Top each patty with a single fried egg and serve hot.

MAUI – MORNING SERVICE

YIELD:
SERVES 4
TIME:
30 MINUTES
V

- 4 large eggs
- 1 cup coconut milk
- 2 teaspoons pure vanilla extract
- ¼ teaspoon kosher salt
- 1 cup finely shredded dried coconut
- 1 tablespoon unsalted butter, for pan
- 8 slices stale brioche

For Serving
Maple syrup

Coconut French Toast

If your morning sweet tooth needs tending, this coconut-crusted French toast is surely the choice for you (though we regret to inform you that Oreo® cookie cake has yet to be added to the breakfast menu). A rich, eggy custard made with coconut milk and a hint of vanilla soaks a lovely brioche, all of which is sealed by a crust of toasted coconut. There's nothing better to start your day. You won't find a more fragrant French toast than this—until your next stay at one of our resorts, of course.

In a small bowl, beat the eggs, coconut milk, vanilla, and salt together until smooth. Pour into a wide, shallow bowl. Place the dried coconut in a similar wide, shallow bowl. Set them next to the stovetop.

Melt the butter in a nonstick skillet or on a griddle over medium heat. It should take about 1 minute for the butter to start foaming. Move it around to completely coat the surface.

While the butter melts, dip a slice of brioche into the egg mixture allowing the mixture to soak into the bread for 5 to 10 seconds on each side. Allow the excess to drip off, then press the bread into the coconut, coating it all around. Gently shake off the excess.

Place the brioche in the pan. Let cook for 3 to 4 minutes, until the coconut is golden. Flip, and cook for 3 to 4 minutes more. (If the coconut browns too quickly, lower the heat to medium-low.) Transfer to a plate kept warm in the oven.

Repeat steps 3 and 4 until you've used up all of the brioche. If your pan can fit two slices, you can cook two at a time. Likewise, if you're using a griddle, cook as many slices as will fit at one time.

Divide the French toast among four plates and serve with maple syrup.

YIELD: SERVES 4
TIME: 1 HOUR
V

- 4 large eggs, separated
- ½ cup whole milk
- 2 teaspoons pure vanilla extract
- 1 cup whole milk ricotta
- 1 teaspoon orange zest
- 3 tablespoons unsalted butter, melted and cooled, plus more for pan
- 1 cup cake flour
- 1½ teaspoons baking powder
- 1 teaspoon baking soda
- ⅓ cup sugar
- 1 teaspoon water

For Serving
Maple syrup

Special Equipment
Stand mixer or handheld mixer

Ricotta Soufflé Pancakes

If ever you catch clouds over The White Lotus in Maui, they're likely to be just as fluffy as our little pancakes. A touch of orange zest adds a burst of sunshine to these otherwise rich, pillowy pancakes, while fragrant vanilla brings a delicate flavor that plays beautifully with the ricotta. These are the kinds of clouds one longs to see every morning. We make them sweeter than normal pancakes, for those of you longing to return to the suite (sweet) life.

In a medium bowl, beat the egg yolks, milk, vanilla, ricotta, and orange zest until smooth. Stream in the butter while whisking continuously, until completely incorporated.

In a small bowl, whisk together the flour, baking powder, baking soda, and sugar. Set aside.

In the bowl of a stand mixer, or in a large bowl with a handheld mixer, beat the egg whites to stiff peaks.

Stir the flour mixture into the egg yolk mixture, until just incorporated, with no dry flour remaining. Scoop one-third of the egg whites into the batter and gently fold in with a spatula until just barely incorporated. Repeat with the remaining egg whites, one-third at a time, until all the egg whites have been incorporated.

Heat about 1 tablespoon of butter in a large nonstick skillet over low heat until foaming. Add about one-eighth of the batter to the skillet, mounding and shaping it into a disk. Drizzle the water into the pan, away from the batter, and cover.

Cook for 5 to 7 minutes, or until you see bubbles forming on top of the pancake. Carefully flip and cook for 2 minutes more.

Repeat with the remaining batter, serving the pancakes as you go, with the maple syrup.

YIELD:
MAKES 12

TIME:
1 HOUR, PLUS
3 HOURS PROOFING

V

- 3 cups bread flour
- 1⅓ cups sugar
- 1 tablespoon instant yeast
- ¾ teaspoon kosher salt
- ½ cup whole milk
- ¼ cup heavy cream
- 2 large eggs
- 3 tablespoons unsalted butter, softened
- 8 cups vegetable or other neutral oil

Special Equipment
Stand mixer with dough hook attachment
6-quart (or larger) Dutch oven
Tongs

Malasadas

These ever-popular donuts are found throughout the Hawaiian islands, but have their origins in Portugal. We start ours with an extra-enriched dough full of eggs, milk, heavy cream, and butter. Think brioche vibes. Don't let the ingredients fool you, though. They're rich, for sure. They're also delicate and soft on the inside, with a light bit of crunch from being rolled in sugar. While these do take some time to make, most of the time is spent hands-off, waiting for the dough to rise, but if you need an excuse to get away from your in-laws, you can always pretend the dough requires your undivided attention.

In the bowl of a stand mixer fitted with the dough hook attachment, whisk together the flour, ⅓ cup of the sugar, yeast, and salt. In a medium bowl, whisk together the milk, heavy cream, and eggs until well combined.

Add the wet mixture to the dry. Mix on low speed until the flour is moistened, then increase the speed to medium. Mix until a soft dough forms, 3 to 5 minutes. Add the butter, 1 tablespoon at a time. Wait until each tablespoon is fully incorporated before adding the next.

Let the mixer run for 5 to 10 minutes more, until the dough is smooth, shiny, and sticky. Grease the inside of a large bowl. Grease your hands, then use your fingers to transfer the dough to the greased bowl. Cover and let rise for 1 to 2 hours, or until doubled in volume.

While the dough rises, cut 12 squares of parchment about 4 by 4 inches. Arrange the squares on a half-sheet pan and spray with cooking spray. Grease a second half-sheet pan.

Grease your hands with cooking spray or oil. Tip the dough out onto the greased half-sheet pan. Knead and spread the dough out into a rectangle about ½ inch thick. Divide the dough into 12 equal portions. Shape each piece into a ½-inch-thick round and set each on a parchment square.

Cover the dough with greased plastic and let sit for 30 to 60 minutes, or until just puffy but not quite doubled in volume. Set a wire cooling rack in the greased half-sheet pan; you'll use this to cool the malasadas, and the pan will catch any excess oil.

Fill a 6-quart Dutch oven an inch from the top with the vegetable oil and heat the oil to 350°F over medium-high heat. When the dough is puffed and the oil is ready, use the parchment squares to lift a dough round and gently place it into the oil parchment-side up.

Repeat with 1 to 3 more dough rounds. A good rule of thumb is to only take up half the surface area of the oil with the donuts. Overcrowding will reduce the oil temperature and lead to greasy donuts. How many you're able to fry at once will depend on the size of your Dutch oven. Use tongs to peel the parchment off the dough after 3 to 4 minutes, or until the oil side is golden. Flip each malasada and fry for 3 to 4 minutes more. Use a wire skimmer to transfer the malasadas to the cooling rack.

Repeat steps 7 and 8 until you've fried all the dough. Check between each batch that the oil remains at 350°F. Let it heat up again before frying more dough, if it has cooled.

Allow the malasadas to cool until you can safely handle them, then roll in the remaining 1 cup of sugar until evenly coated. Serve warm or at room temperature. Malasadas are best eaten the day they're made.

YIELD:
MAKES 8

TIME:
30 MINUTES

One 12-ounce can Spam®

1 teaspoon vegetable or other neutral oil

2 tablespoons soy sauce

2 tablespoons maple syrup

1 teaspoon toasted sesame oil

1 tablespoon furikake (optional)

4 cups cooked short-grain white rice

3 sheets nori, cut into 2-inch-wide strips

Special Equipment
Musubi mold kit (see Note)

Spam Musubi

This is a must-have for anybody visiting the islands because it's a specialty and favorite among many locals here. Spam Musubi is an exquisite blend of sweet and salty that satisfies every single time. Our chefs tried all sorts of variations but, in the end, settled on something fairly close to the classic. Instead of brown sugar, we sweeten ours with maple syrup, and we add a touch of sesame oil for a toasty nuttiness that sings when paired with the crispy pan-fried Spam. Consider a little sprinkle of furikake (a delectable seasoning blend from Japan) between the Spam and rice to add texture and nuanced flavor. We like it both with and without—you decide what's best for you.

Cut the Spam into 8 equal slices. Heat the oil in a large nonstick skillet over medium heat. Lay the Spam in the pan in a single layer. Cook for 3 to 4 minutes on each side, or until crisp.

Decrease the heat to medium-low and add the soy sauce, maple syrup, and sesame oil to the pan. Swirl them in the pan, and then flip the Spam slices. Cook until the sauce is reduced and sticky and clinging to the Spam, 1 to 2 minutes. Remove the pan from the heat and transfer the Spam to a plate; let cool slightly.

Fill a small bowl with warm water. Place a slice of Spam into the musubi mold. Sprinkle a couple pinches of furikake on top, if using.

Dip your hands in the warm water. Scoop about ½ cup of rice into the mold and press it down just hard enough for the rice to hold the shape of the mold. (Pressing too hard will result in a dense musubi.)

Wrap the molded Spam and rice tightly with a strip of nori, so that the ends meet on the bottom of the rice. With damp fingers, press the ends together to stick them to the rice. Repeat with the remaining ingredients. Serve immediately.

 NOTE

If you don't have or want to buy a musubi mold, you can just use a clean Spam can lined with plastic wrap. Fill the can as instructed, compress using the overhanging plastic wrap, then use the plastic wrap to lift the musubi out.

YIELD:
SERVES 4 TO 6

TIME:
15 MINUTES, PLUS 24 HOURS RESTING

GF

- 1 pound skin-on salmon fillets
- 1 tablespoon kosher salt
- 4 large plum tomatoes, seeded and diced
- 1 small sweet onion, minced
- 1 tablespoon fresh lime juice
- ½ teaspoon black pepper
- 1 to 2 scallions, finely sliced (optional)

Lomi Lomi Salmon

Lomi lomi is a Hawaiian phrase meaning "rub" or "massage." You may have noticed that our spa offers a particular treatment called a lomi lomi massage. Our caregiving teams know just how to work out your aches, pains, and stress. Similarly, our chefs know to gently, lovingly massage salt-cured salmon with fresh tomatoes and onions and a few simple seasonings. The end result is a delightfully salty, tangy dish that many serve as a side to kalua pig and other traditional Hawaiian fare.

Line a large plate with plastic wrap. Pat the salmon dry with paper towels and rub all over with the salt. Place on the plate and wrap in the plastic wrap. Refrigerate for 24 hours.

Rinse the salmon with cold water and pat dry with paper towels. Remove and discard the skin. Dice the salmon and transfer to a large bowl.

Add the tomatoes, onions, lime juice, and pepper. Use your hands to gently toss and massage the ingredients until well combined. Serve cold as a side dish with roast pork (like kalua pig) or other dishes. This dish is typically served as is, but you may consider topping with finely sliced scallions, to taste.

YIELD:
MAKES 12

TIME:
5 HOURS

Filling
2 pounds boneless pork shoulder, cut into 3-inch cubes

⅓ cup packed dark brown sugar

¼ cup soy sauce

½ cup pineapple juice

¼ cup sake

1½ teaspoons Chinese five spice powder

2 cloves garlic, minced

1 tablespoon cornstarch

1 tablespoon water

1 to 2 tablespoons hoisin sauce

Dough
2 cups all-purpose flour, plus more for rolling

1 tablespoon granulated sugar

1½ teaspoons instant yeast

1 teaspoon baking powder

½ teaspoon kosher salt

1 cup lukewarm water

1 teaspoon vegetable or other neutral oil, plus more for bowl

1 large egg whisked with 1 tablespoon water (for egg wash, if baking)

Special Equipment
Stand mixer with dough hook attachment

Bamboo steamer and large wok (if steaming)

Manapua

This classic Hawaiian dish encapsulates a grab-and-go style of eating—perfect for guests with a busy day planned. Steamed or baked, manapua can be prepared with many different fillings, but the quintessential version uses char siu–style pork. We stuff our manapua with slow-roasted pork shoulder for a succulent, sticky filling that satisfies with every bite. We provide options for baking or steaming, because the process is the same right up until it's time to cook the buns.

To make the filling and dough: Preheat the oven to 300°F.

Place the pork in a 9-by-9-inch baking dish. In a small saucepan, combine the brown sugar, soy sauce, pineapple juice, sake, five spice, and garlic. Cook over low heat, stirring constantly, just until the sugar has dissolved.

Pour the mixture over the pork and toss until well coated. Cover with aluminum foil and bake until the pork pulls apart with a fork, 3 to 4 hours. Remove the pork, reserving the liquid. Shred the pork and set aside.

Pour the liquid into a bowl or measuring cup and chill until the fat solidifies. Discard the fat and reserve ¾ cup of the liquid.

In the bowl of a stand mixer fitted with the dough hook attachment, combine the flour, granulated sugar, yeast, baking powder, and salt. Mix on low speed until combined, then add the lukewarm water and the oil. Continue mixing until the flour is moistened, then increase the speed to medium and mix until the dough is smooth and elastic, about 10 minutes.

Grease a bowl with oil. Transfer the dough to the bowl and turn to coat. Cover and let rise until doubled in volume, about 1 hour.

While the dough rises, combine the cornstarch and 1 tablespoon water in a medium saucepan. Stir until uniform. Add the reserved cooking liquid. Heat over medium, stirring constantly, until thickened and boiling, 5 to 7 minutes.

Remove from the heat and stir in the shredded pork. Add the hoisin sauce to taste. Let cool to room temperature.

Turn the dough out onto a lightly oiled work surface and divide into 12 equal portions. Roll into balls. Working one at a time, flatten each ball into a disk while keeping the remaining balls covered with plastic or a clean tea towel to prevent them from drying out. The centers should be about ¼ inch thick, tapering to ⅛ inch at the edges (the edges will be the seams at the bottom of the buns).

Continued on page 26.

Manapua Continued

To assemble the buns: Mound 2 to 3 tablespoons of pork (you may not use all of the filling) in the center of a disk. Fold over the edges to make a pocket and pinch the edges to seal closed. Repeat the process with the remaining dough disks and cover the filled buns with lightly greased plastic wrap. Let rise for 30 minutes, until puffy.

If steaming, transfer the buns, seam-side down, to a bamboo steamer basket lined with parchment paper (4 buns per tier of the basket). Fill a large wok with a couple of inches of water, enough to just barely reach the bottom of the steamer basket. Bring to a boil over high heat. Steam for 7 to 10 minutes, until cooked through.

Optional: If baking, transfer to a half-sheet pan lined with parchment paper, seam-side down (you can fit all 12 on the same pan). Preheat the oven to 375°F. Brush the buns with the egg wash. Bake for 18 to 20 minutes, until golden brown.

Let the buns cool slightly before serving them hot.

YIELD:
SERVES 2

TIME:
25 MINUTES

- 1 pound jumbo EZ-peel shrimp
- 2 tablespoons all-purpose flour
- ¾ teaspoon kosher salt
- 2 teaspoons smoked paprika
- 1 teaspoon lemon zest
- ½ teaspoon black pepper
- ¼ teaspoon cayenne
- 6 tablespoons unsalted butter
- 20 cloves garlic, minced
- 2 tablespoons extra virgin olive oil
- 1 tablespoon minced parsley
- 2 tablespoons fresh lemon juice

For Serving
- 2 cups cooked short-grain white rice

Garlic Shrimp

Garlic only begins to describe the flavor of these shrimp. From homes to food trucks to restaurants all around the island, everyone has their own take on these delicious shrimp. Yes, garlic is the star of the show, but don't forget the cast of supporting players like smoky paprika, tangy lemon, and a burst of warmth from cayenne. For those celebrating a honeymoon, this dish serves two, and who can complain if you *both* have garlic breath?

Pat the shrimp dry with paper towels and transfer them to a large bowl. Dust with the flour, salt, paprika, lemon zest, black pepper, and cayenne. Toss until evenly coated. Set aside.

In a large skillet over medium-low heat, melt the butter. Swirl the pan occasionally, until the butter begins to foam. Add the garlic and cook, stirring constantly, until the garlic just begins to brown and crisp, 3 to 5 minutes. Transfer to a bowl and set aside.

In a large skillet over medium heat, heat the oil. Add half the shrimp and cook, undisturbed, for 2 to 3 minutes, or until pink and just starting to sear on the shells. Flip the shrimp and cook for 2 to 3 minutes longer, until cooked through. Transfer to a bowl and repeat with the remaining shrimp. Add more oil to the pan if needed.

Once the second batch of shrimp is cooked, return the first batch and the garlic butter to the pan. Toss just until the shrimp is completely coated. Add the parsley and lemon juice, tossing to coat. Divide the rice between two plates, and cover each with an equal portion of the shrimp. Serve immediately.

28 MAUI – MORNING SERVICE

YIELD: SERVES 2
TIME: 20 MINUTES

- 1 teaspoon dried wakame
- 2 tablespoons mayonnaise
- 1 to 2 teaspoons sriracha
- 8 ounces sushi-grade tuna, diced
- 1 tablespoon soy sauce
- 1 teaspoon sesame oil
- ½ teaspoon mixed sesame seeds, plus more for garnish
- 1 large carrot, peeled
- 1 Persian cucumber
- ½ cup cooked and shelled edamame
- ¼ teaspoon shichimi togarashi
- Salt
- 1 avocado
- ½ cup diced pineapple, preferably fresh

For Serving
- 2 cups cooked short-grain white rice

Poke Bowl

This Hawaiian staple is as varied as it is ubiquitous, customizable to your heart's delight. We start with the classic tuna for our version, gently tossed with salty, umami-rich soy sauce and delicately nutty sesame oil. The rest is a blend of fresh vegetables, fruit, and spicy edamame, all drizzled with spicy mayonnaise. Mix the ingredients for a blend of flavors, or keep them separate and mix and match as you please—there's no wrong way to enjoy a good poke.

Crumble the wakame into smaller bits, then transfer to a small bowl. Cover with 2 inches of cold water and set aside until rehydrated, about 5 minutes. Drain.

In a small bowl, combine the mayonnaise and sriracha to taste and mix until integrated. (Start with 1 teaspoon of sriracha, taste, and add more as desired.) Transfer to a resealable sandwich bag, seal (pushing the air out), and refrigerate until ready to use.

In a large bowl, combine the tuna, soy sauce, sesame oil, sesame seeds, and rehydrated wakame. Toss until completely combined, cover with plastic wrap, and refrigerate while you prepare the remaining ingredients.

Shred the carrot on a box grater using the largest holes. Thinly slice the cucumber. In a bowl, toss the edamame, shichimi togarashi, and a large pinch of salt. Halve, pit, and thinly slice the avocado.

Divide the rice between two bowls. Divide the tuna mixture between each, mounding it in the center of the bowl. Divide the carrot, cucumber, edamame, avocado, and pineapple between the bowls, arranging each element around the outside of the tuna.

Snip a corner off the sandwich bag containing the spicy mayo and drizzle the mayonnaise in a zigzag pattern over the top of both bowls. Sprinkle with additional sesame seeds and serve.

YIELD:
SERVES 4 TO 6
TIME:
30 MINUTES
GF

- ¼ cup unsalted butter
- 1 medium yellow onion, finely diced
- 2 medium carrots, peeled and diced
- 2 stalks celery, diced
- 2 teaspoons grated ginger
- 1 teaspoon grated garlic
- 1½ teaspoons kosher salt
- ½ teaspoon black pepper
- 3 medium Yukon gold potatoes, cut into 1-inch cubes
- 1 cup frozen fire-roasted corn
- Two 13.5-ounce cans coconut milk
- 8 ounces boneless, skinless cod fillets, cut into bite-size pieces
- 16 medium shrimp, peeled and deveined
- 16 sea scallops
- 8 ounces cooked lobster meat, coarsely chopped
- 2 tablespoons fresh lime juice

Special Equipment
Dutch oven

EVENING SERVICE

Coconut Seafood Chowder

This sumptuous chowder is inspired by a mix of some of the best catches of the day from our local fishermen, with a bit of influence from different cuisines. It's not unlike a New England–style chowder, but with some aromatics that meld nicely with the coconut milk, like ginger, garlic, and lime juice. The sweetness of the fire-roasted corn pairs well with the natural richness of the coconut milk and shellfish. The result is a well-balanced bowl of chowder, full of decadent seafood and a creamy, fragrant broth. This is one of many options available on our *fairly* private and *entirely romantic* evening boat tours.

In a large Dutch oven over medium heat, heat the butter until melted and foaming. Add the onion, carrots, and celery and cook, stirring occasionally, for 5 to 7 minutes or until softened. Add the ginger, garlic, salt, and pepper and cook, stirring constantly, until fragrant, about 1 minute.

Add the potatoes, corn, and coconut milk. Increase the heat to high and bring to a boil, then decrease to a simmer. Cook, stirring occasionally, until the potatoes are fork-tender, 10 to 15 minutes.

Add the cod, shrimp, and scallops. Simmer just until cooked through and opaque, 3 to 5 minutes. Stir in the lobster meat and cook until warmed through. Season to taste with salt and pepper. Remove from the heat, stir in the lime juice, and serve immediately.

YIELD:
SERVES 4

TIME:
90 MINUTES, PLUS 4 TO 8 HOURS MARINATING

Marinade
4 cups water
½ cup soy sauce
½ cup pineapple juice
¼ cup fresh lime juice
1 tablespoon lime zest
1 tablespoon grated ginger
2 teaspoons grated garlic
One 4- to 6-pound chicken, spatchcocked (see Note)

Glaze
1½ cups pineapple juice
½ cup ketchup
⅓ cup soy sauce
¼ cup sake
2 tablespoons yuzu or fresh lime juice
¼ cup packed light brown sugar
1 tablespoon grated ginger
1 teaspoon grated garlic
1 teaspoon black pepper

For Serving
8 pineapple slices
4 red bell peppers, trimmed, seeded, and cut into 2-inch-wide strips
Salt

Special Equipment
Gas or charcoal grill
Applewood or cherrywood chips (optional)
Cooking thermometer

Huli Huli Chicken

This Hawaiian barbecue chicken gets a double dose of flavor from a stint in a marinade of fragrant aromatics, followed by a generous basting with a glaze. Part teriyaki, part barbecue sauce, this glaze also has elements of the marinade in it to make each bite a sweet, savory, tangy triumph. For an additional layer of smokiness, try adding applewood or cherrywood to your grill's coals. For those reluctant to invest in four to eight hours of marinating time first, consider this: That's four to eight hours you can relax by the pool and contemplate your career path.

To make the marinade: In a large bowl, combine the water, soy sauce, pineapple juice, lime juice, lime zest, ginger, and garlic. Stir until completely combined. Place the chicken in a large, resealable freezer bag and pour in the marinade. Seal the bag, squeezing out any excess air. Place the bag in a bowl or on a tray, then refrigerate for at least 4 hours, and up to 8 hours.

To make the glaze: In a medium saucepan, combine the pineapple juice, ketchup, soy sauce, sake, yuzu juice, brown sugar, ginger, garlic, and black pepper. Bring to a boil over medium-high heat, stirring constantly. Boil until the glaze is reduced and thick enough to coat the back of a spoon, 7 to 10 minutes. Let cool, and then refrigerate until ready to use.

To make the chicken: Prepare a gas or charcoal grill for two-zone heating (either by lighting half the burners or by lighting the charcoal in a chimney starter and dumping it so that it only fills half the grill). While the grill heats, drain the marinade from the bag and pat the chicken dry with paper towels.

Place the chicken, breast-side up, on the cool side of the grill (not over the flames or coals), with the legs pointing toward the hot zone.

Optional: For a smoky flavor, throw some applewood or cherrywood chips or chunks onto the coals (or add wood chips to a smoking tray for a gas grill). Cover and smoke the chicken for about 30 minutes.

Check the internal temperature of the chicken with a probe thermometer stuck in the thickest part of the thigh. Once the internal temperature reaches 150°F, start basting the chicken with the glaze every 3 minutes or so. Flip and baste the other side. Continue basting until the internal temperature reaches 165°F. The chicken should take 45 to 60 minutes to cook and glaze.

Transfer the chicken to a cutting board and let rest for 10 to 15 minutes before carving and serving. While the chicken rests, grill the pineapple slices and pepper strips on the hot side of the grill until charred and the peppers are slightly softened, about 3 minutes on each side. Season the peppers with salt to taste and serve with the chicken.

NOTE

If your grocery store or butcher doesn't sell chickens pre-spatchcocked, you can ask the folks at the butcher counter to do it for you. Otherwise, place the chicken breast-side down on a cutting board and use a good pair of kitchen shears to remove the backbone (cut along both sides of it, a little at a time, to make it a bit easier). Flip the chicken breast-side up and press down to break the breastbone and make the chicken lie flat, then proceed with the recipe.

YIELD:
SERVES 4

TIME:
45 MINUTES

Mahi Mahi
3 tablespoons soy sauce
1 tablespoon sesame oil
1 tablespoon grated ginger
1 tablespoon fresh lime juice
1 teaspoon lime zest
½ teaspoon black pepper
Four 4-ounce mahi mahi fillets
½ cup sesame seeds
2 tablespoons olive oil, plus more for coating fish

Purée
3 cups frozen shelled edamame
½ bunch cilantro, chopped (leaves and tender stems only)
2 teaspoons grated ginger
1 tablespoon fresh lime juice
1 teaspoon kosher salt
¼ teaspoon black pepper
¼ teaspoon shichimi togarashi
3 tablespoons olive oil
1 tablespoon sesame oil

For Serving
Lime wedges
Microgreens or cilantro
Sesame oil

Special Equipment
Blender
Fine-mesh strainer

Seared Sesame-Crusted Mahi Mahi

The mahi mahi we serve is all sourced from local fishermen, right off the coast, mere miles from the resort. The word *mahi mahi* comes from the Hawaiian word for "strong," even though it's a mild-flavored fish. We suspect strong refers to the fish themselves, which you can find out for yourself if you'd like! Just book a fishing charter with the concierge in the lobby. Otherwise, feel free to enjoy local mahi mahi in a different way, crusted with sesame seeds and served on a luscious bed of puréed edamame.

To make the mahi mahi: In a small bowl, combine the soy sauce, sesame oil, ginger, lime juice, lime zest, and pepper. Whisk until completely combined. Arrange the mahi mahi fillets in a shallow baking dish and pour the marinade over the fish. Cover and refrigerate for 30 minutes, flipping once.

To make the purée: Bring a large pot of water to a boil over high heat. Add the edamame and boil for 5 to 7 minutes, or until tender. Drain, reserving about 1 cup of the water.

In a blender, combine the edamame, cilantro, ginger, lime juice, salt, pepper, and shichimi togarashi. Add about ¼ cup of the reserved cooking liquid and blend on low speed until the purée starts to come together. Increase the speed to medium-high and drizzle in the olive oil and sesame oil while blending. Blend until smooth, adding a splash of water as needed if the purée is too thick. Taste and adjust the seasonings as necessary.

Transfer the purée to a fine-mesh strainer set over a small saucepan. Press the purée through the strainer with a rubber spatula, discarding any solid bits. Heat the strained purée over low heat, just to keep warm. Stir occasionally.

Remove the mahi mahi from the marinade and pat dry with paper towels. Add the sesame seeds to a shallow bowl. Brush the mahi mahi with olive oil, then dredge each fillet in the sesame seeds, until coated all over.

Heat the olive oil in a large skillet over medium-high heat until shimmering. Add the mahi mahi fillets and cook for 1 minute before lowering the heat to medium. Cook until golden brown, about 3 minutes. Flip, then cook for 3 to 5 minutes, until golden brown on the other side.

While the fish is searing, spoon the purée onto four plates. Gently spread it into an oblong shape a bit larger than the fish fillets. Top with a fillet, and garnish with a lime wedge and fresh microgreens or cilantro. Drizzle with sesame oil around the outside of the purée. Serve immediately.

YIELD:
SERVES 4

TIME:
90 MINUTES

Pork Chops
Four 6-ounce thick-cut, boneless pork chops
1 tablespoon hot honey, warmed
1½ teaspoons kosher salt
½ teaspoon black pepper
2 cloves garlic
1 teaspoon fresh rosemary leaves
1 cup macadamia nuts, toasted and cooled
¼ teaspoon ground mustard
¼ teaspoon sweet paprika
1 cup panko
2 tablespoons olive oil
2 tablespoons unsalted butter

Roasted Vegetables
3 cups Brussels sprouts, trimmed and halved
2 medium sweet potatoes, peeled and cut to 1½-inch chunks
2 tablespoons olive oil
1 teaspoon sweet paprika
½ teaspoon kosher salt
¼ teaspoon ground mustard
¼ teaspoon black pepper

Special Equipment
Food processor
Stainless steel or cast-iron skillet
Cooking thermometer

Macadamia-Crusted Pork

Take thick-cut, juicy pork chops and coat them in a crust of breadcrumbs, herbs, and finely crushed macadamia nuts, and what have you got? A fine meal. Food is no joke at The White Lotus and this dish is no exception—it's almost as popular as our Pineapple Suite! Because we start with thick-cut pork chops, a quick sear in the pan and a finish in the oven is the best way to avoid burning that delicious, buttery crust.

To make the pork chops: Preheat the oven to 450°F. Place the racks at the upper and middle positions. Line a half-sheet pan with parchment paper.

Pat the pork chops dry with paper towels, then brush all over with the hot honey. Season all over with the salt and pepper, then set aside.

Pulse the garlic and rosemary in a food processor until fine. Add the macadamia nuts, mustard, and paprika. Pulse until the nuts are finely ground and similar in texture to the panko. Add the panko and pulse just to combine.

Transfer the breading mix to a large shallow dish. Dredge the pork chops all over, pressing them into the breading until completely coated. Reserve any remaining breadcrumbs.

To make the roasted vegetables: In a large bowl, combine the Brussels sprouts and sweet potatoes, drizzle with the olive oil, and toss to coat. Dust with the paprika, salt, ground mustard, and pepper. Toss to coat and transfer to the prepared half-sheet pan. Roast in the oven on the upper rack for 15 minutes.

While the vegetables roast, heat the olive oil for the pork chops in a large stainless steel or cast-iron skillet (the skillet must be oven-safe) over medium-high heat until shimmering.

Lay the pork chops in the pan and sear until golden, 2 to 4 minutes on each side. When you've seared both sides, hold the pork chops with tongs and sear the edges, 1 to 2 minutes.

Transfer the pork chops to a plate and lower the oven temperature to 400°F (when the vegetables have roasted for 15 minutes).

Place the skillet with the pork chops on the lower rack. Toss the vegetables to ensure an even browning. Roast the pork chops for 7 to 12 minutes, or until the internal temperature registers 150° to 155°F for medium, 155° to 160°F for medium-well, and 165°F for well-done.

Transfer the pork chops to a cutting board. Tent loosely with aluminum foil and let rest for 10 to 15 minutes. Meanwhile, test the vegetables—if they are fork-tender and golden, remove from the oven and cover to keep warm while the pork rests. (If they aren't fork-tender, roast for 5 to 10 minutes more, while the pork rests.)

In a small nonstick skillet, heat the butter over medium heat until foaming. Add the reserved breadcrumbs and cook, stirring occasionally, until golden brown and crisp.

To serve: Divide the roasted vegetables among four plates. Add a pork chop to each plate, and top with the pan-seared breadcrumbs. Serve hot.

MAUI — EVENING SERVICE

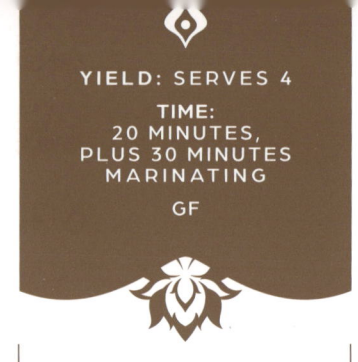

YIELD: SERVES 4
TIME:
20 MINUTES, PLUS 30 MINUTES MARINATING
GF

Pineapple-Orange Pico de Gallo
4 large plum tomatoes, diced
¼ cup finely chopped fresh pineapple
¼ cup chopped Cara Cara orange (membranes removed)
1 small sweet onion, minced
1 jalapeño, trimmed, seeded, and minced
Juice of 1 lime
½ teaspoon kosher salt
¼ bunch cilantro, finely chopped

Mahi Mahi
1 pound skinless mahi mahi, swordfish, or cod fillets
1 tablespoon olive oil
1 tablespoon fresh lime juice
¾ teaspoon kosher salt
½ teaspoon ground coriander
½ teaspoon ground cumin
¼ teaspoon smoked paprika
¼ teaspoon black pepper
Vegetable oil, for brushing

For Serving
8 corn tortillas, warmed
2 avocados, peeled, pitted, and sliced

Special Equipment
Gas or charcoal grill (or broiler)

Fish Tacos

Sometimes, simple and fresh is best. These fish tacos are a testament to that idea. They celebrate both local produce and local fish—mahi mahi caught fresh from nearby waters and a delicious, tangy salsa made with pineapples grown on the island. All of that goodness is deliciously encased in soft corn tortillas. For guests more accustomed to mainland fish tacos, where the fish is battered and deep-fried, it's worth mentioning that we opt for grilling the fish. A broiler will work just as well. When preparing this one at home, feel free to replace the mahi mahi with another fish that swims near your waters, perhaps swordfish or cod?

To make the pico de gallo: In a medium bowl, combine the tomatoes, pineapple, orange, onion, jalapeño, lime juice, salt, and cilantro. Toss until all the ingredients are evenly coated and thoroughly mixed. Taste and adjust the seasoning with more salt or lime juice, as desired. Cover and refrigerate until ready to use.

To make the mahi mahi: Pat the mahi mahi fillets dry with paper towels and transfer to a plate. In a small bowl, combine the olive oil, lime juice, salt, coriander, cumin, paprika, and black pepper and whisk until smooth. Massage the fillets with the marinade. Cover and refrigerate for 30 minutes, flipping once.

Prepare a gas or charcoal grill for medium-high heat (or preheat a broiler). Brush the grates with vegetable oil.

Grill or broil the fish for 3 to 5 minutes on each side, until well seared and lightly charred in some spots. Transfer to a cutting board and tent with foil. Let rest for 5 to 10 minutes, then cut into chunks.

Divide the chunks of grilled fish among the tortillas. Top each with a spoonful of the pico de gallo and 2 or 3 slices of avocado. Serve immediately.

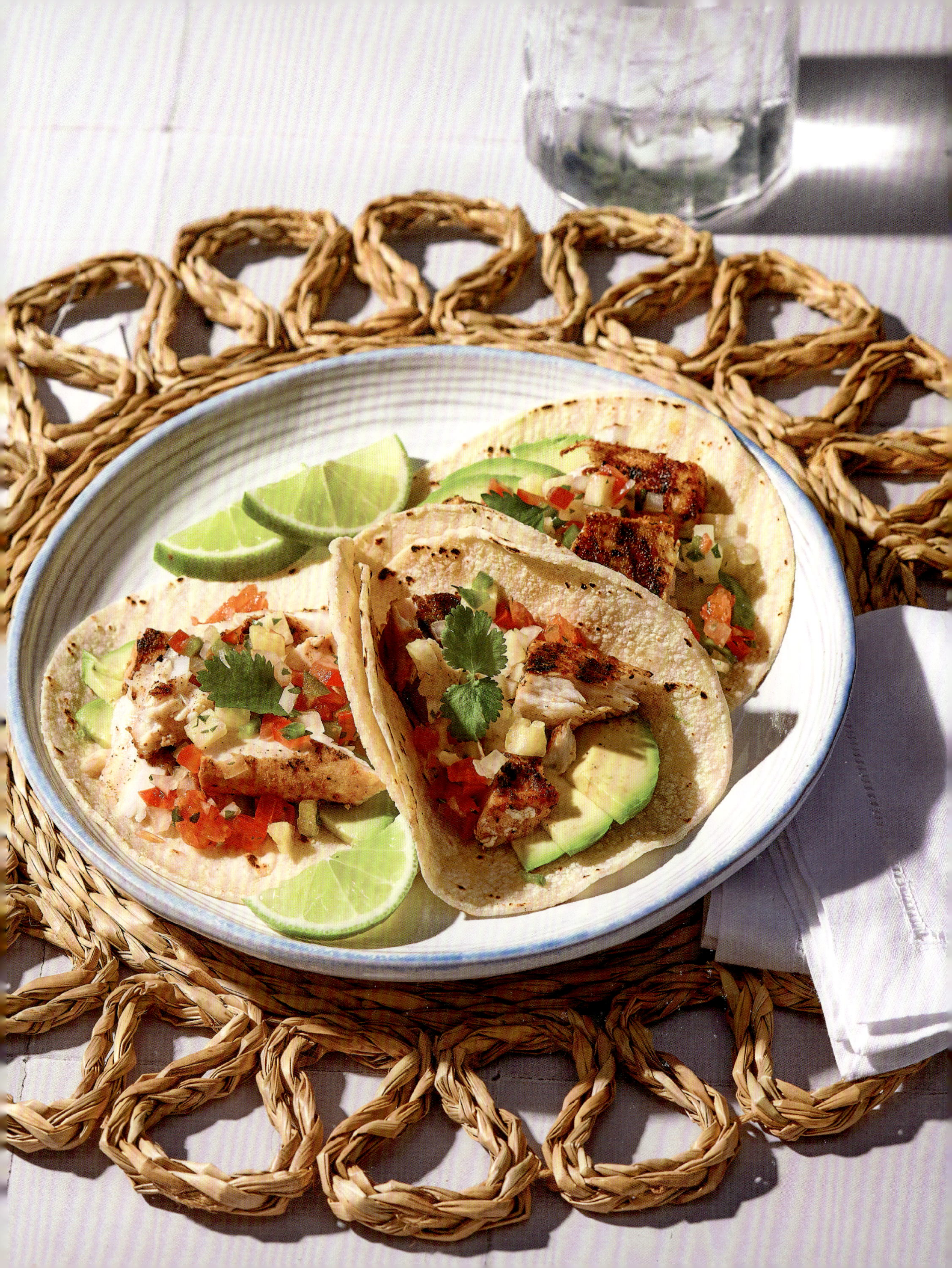

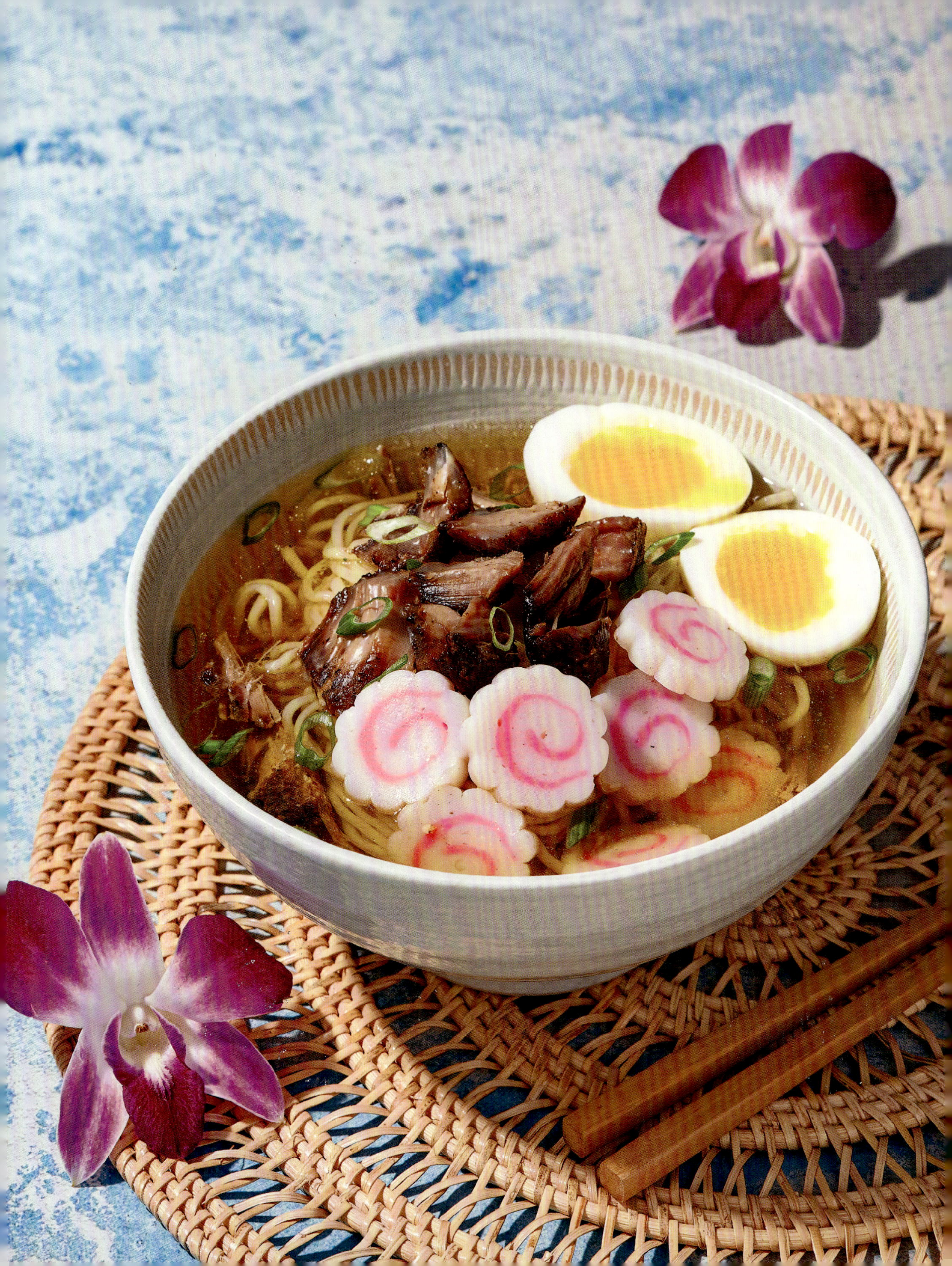

YIELD:
SERVES 4

TIME:
5 HOURS

Kalua Pig
1½ pounds boneless pork shoulder, cut into 2-inch cubes

½ teaspoon kosher salt

½ teaspoon black pepper

1 tablespoon vegetable or other neutral oil

2 tablespoons soy sauce

¼ teaspoon liquid smoke (optional)

Dashi Broth
8 cups chicken stock

1 ounce dried shiitake mushrooms

1 ounce dried shrimp

1 large carrot, coarsely chopped

1 small yellow onion, quartered

One 2-inch piece ginger, sliced

One 4-inch piece kombu seaweed

1 tablespoon instant dashi powder

For Assembly
4 portions ramen or saimin noodles

4 soft-boiled eggs, peeled and halved

2 ounces kamaboko (fish cake), cut into thin slices

Scallions, thinly sliced

Special Equipment
8-by-8-inch or 9-by-9-inch baking dish

Saimin

Saimin is a beautiful fusion of different noodle dishes, like ramen chow mein, Poke Bowls (page 31), and Spam Musubi (page 21). It is one of the more ubiquitous dishes found in Hawaiian eateries. It's such a popular food item that it has even made appearances on national fast food chain menus. Though, of course, we think we can do better than that, especially when it comes to ambience. Ours starts as most do, with a simple dashi broth. But we add an oven-baked preparation of kalua pig as the protein (though ham or chashu are also common options).

To make the kalua pig: Preheat the oven to 325°F.

In a 8-by-8-inch or 9-by-9-inch baking dish, combine the pork, salt, pepper, oil, soy sauce, and liquid smoke (if using). Toss until evenly coated. Cover with foil and bake until the pork is fork-tender, 3 to 4 hours.

To make the dashi broth: When the pork is about halfway done, prepare the broth. In a large pot, combine the stock, mushrooms, shrimp, carrot, onion, ginger, and kombu. Bring to a boil over high heat, then decrease to a simmer. Cook, covered, for 1 hour.

Strain the broth and discard the solids. Return the liquid to the pot and stir in the dashi powder. Keep warm over low heat.

Remove the cooked pork from the oven, drain the liquid, and shred the pork.

To assemble: Bring a large pot of water to a boil over high heat. Cook the ramen according to the package instructions. Drain and divide the noodles among four large noodle bowls.

Add about 2 cups of dashi broth to each bowl. Divide the shredded pork among the bowls and top each bowl with two egg halves and slices of kamaboko, to taste. Sprinkle with scallions and serve.

MAUI — EVENING SERVICE

YIELD:
SERVES 2

TIME:
30 MINUTES

Miso Butter
2 tablespoons unsalted butter, softened
1 teaspoon white miso
1 teaspoon red miso
½ teaspoon grated ginger

Steaks
Two 6-ounce boneless rib-eye steaks
2 teaspoons olive oil
½ teaspoon kosher salt
½ teaspoon black pepper

Sautéed Mushrooms
2 tablespoons olive oil
8 ounces shiitake mushrooms
¼ teaspoon kosher salt
¼ teaspoon black pepper
1 tablespoon unsalted butter
1 teaspoon soy sauce

Special Equipment
Cooking Thermometer

Seared Steak with Shiitake Mushrooms and Miso Butter

It may surprise you to discover that we prefer to start our steaks in a cold pan when we're not grilling them. One of our signatures is this gentle spin on a steakhouse classic of rib eye and mushrooms. We opt for meaty shiitake mushrooms well sautéed until crisp at the edges and a compound butter using both red and white miso. We use the former for its deep umami flavors and the latter for its sweetness.

To make the miso butter: In a small bowl, combine the butter, white and red miso, and ginger. Stir until thoroughly blended. Set aside.

To make the steaks: Pat the steaks dry with paper towels. Brush them all over with the oil (a thin layer is all you need). Season with salt and pepper and transfer to a cold, large nonstick skillet.

Heat the skillet over high heat for 3 minutes. Flip the steaks and cook for 2 minutes more. Lower the heat to medium and continue cooking the steaks, flipping every 2 minutes, until a dark crust forms and the meat reaches the desired doneness (130° to 135°F for medium-rare, 135° to 145°F for medium, 145° to 150°F for medium-well, and 165°F for well-done). Transfer to a cutting board and tent with foil. Let rest for 15 minutes while you prepare the mushrooms.

To make the mushrooms: In a large skillet over medium-high heat, heat the oil until shimmering. Add the mushrooms, salt, and pepper. Cook, stirring occasionally, until the mushrooms are golden and turning crisp at the edges, 10 to 12 minutes. Add the butter and soy sauce, tossing to coat for 2 to 3 minutes, until glazed and the mushrooms look shiny and well coated. Remove from heat.

Divide the mushrooms between two plates, creating a small bed for the steaks. Top the mushrooms with the rested seared steaks. Just before serving, top each steak with half the miso butter (use a 1-tablespoon cookie scoop or measuring spoon to create a nice, rounded scoop of butter, if desired). Serve hot.

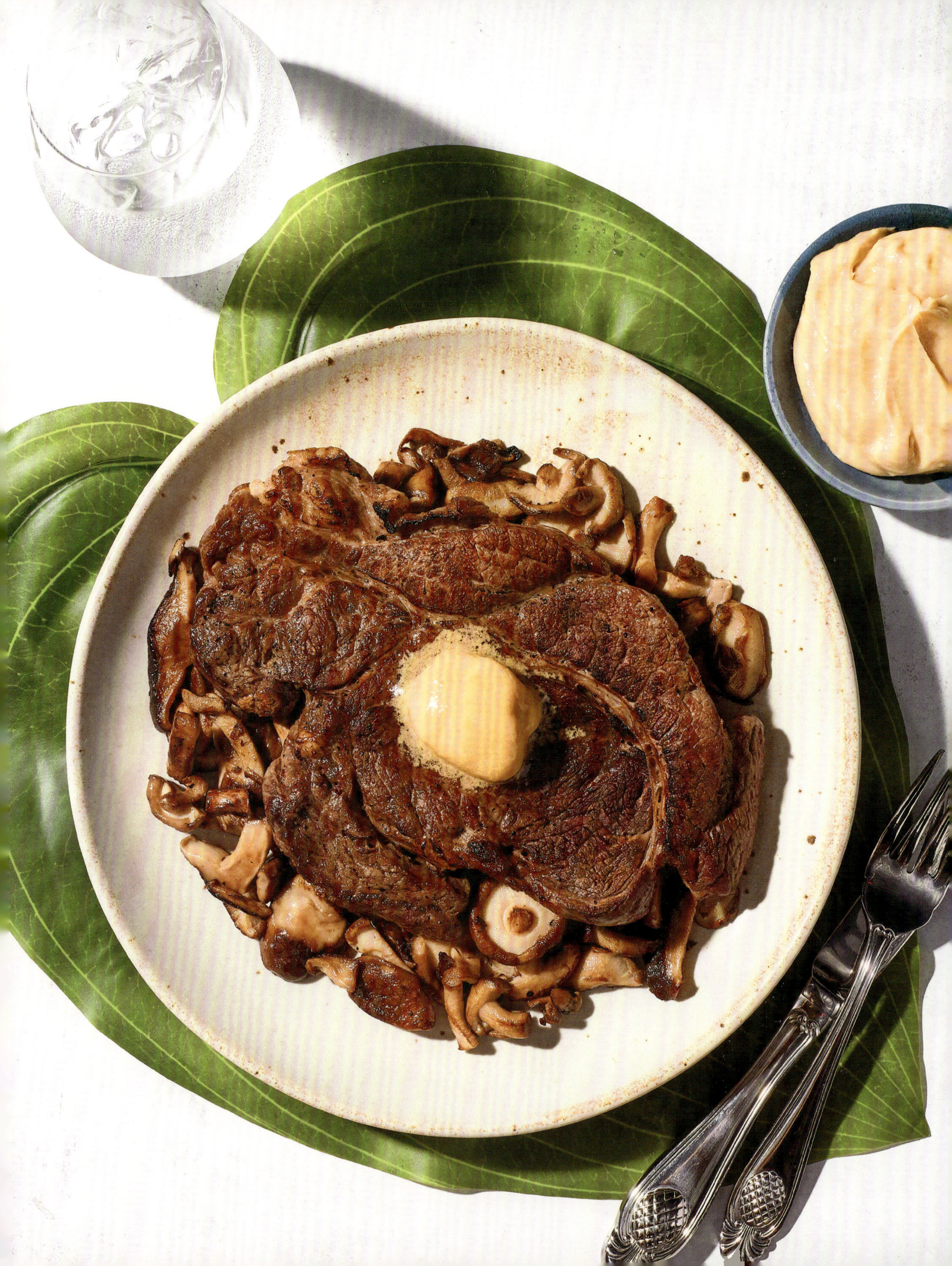

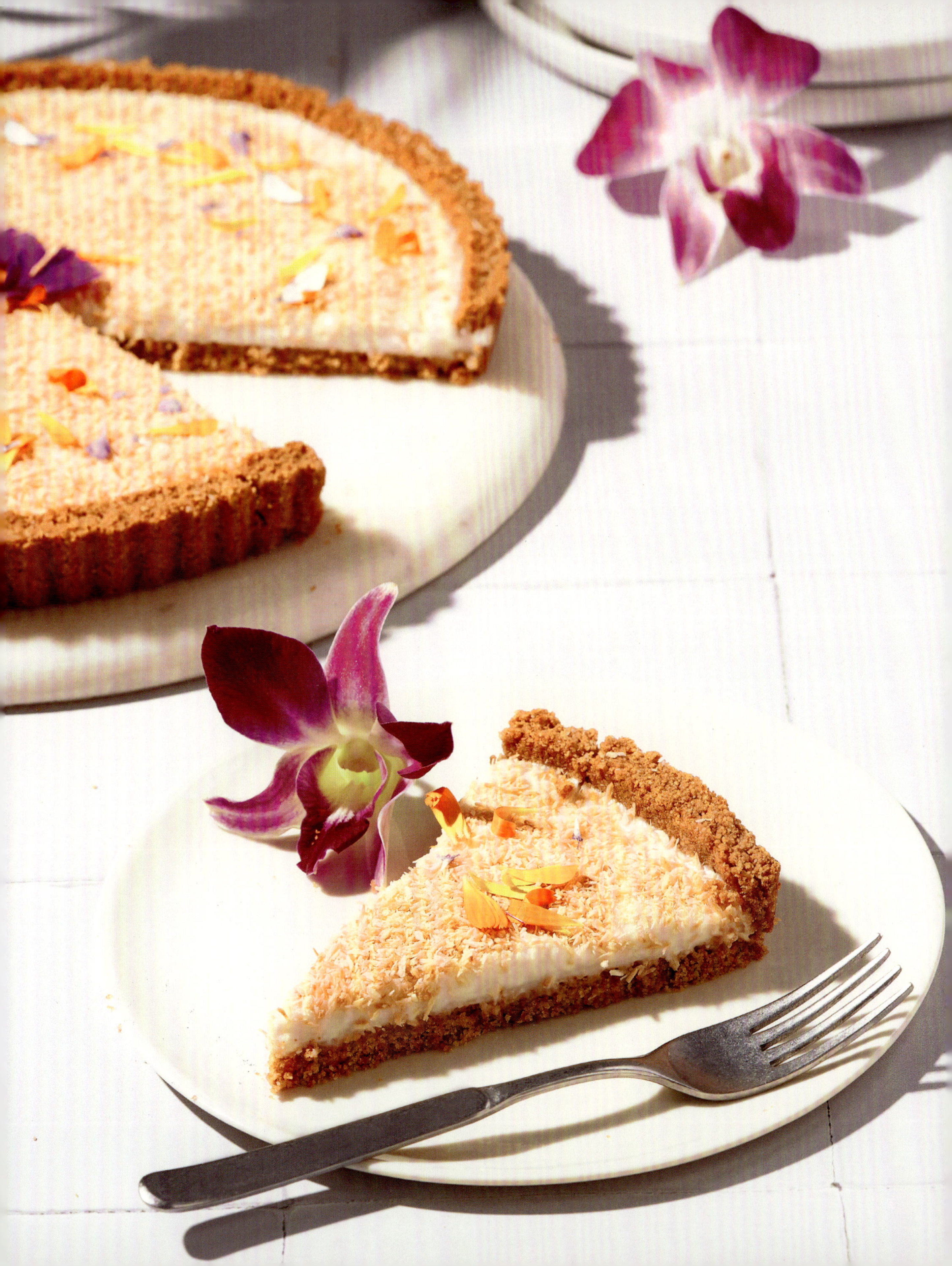

YIELD:
SERVES 8 TO 12

TIME:
35 MINUTES, PLUS 4 HOURS TO SET

V

Crust
- One 5.3-ounce box shortbread cookies
- 3 ounces gingersnaps (3 or 4 cookies)
- ½ cup unsalted macadamia nuts
- ¼ teaspoon kosher salt
- ¼ cup unsalted butter, melted and cooled

Filling
- ¼ cup sugar
- 3 tablespoons cornstarch
- 1 cup whole milk
- 1 cup coconut milk
- 2 teaspoons pure vanilla extract
- ½ teaspoon coconut extract

For Assembly
- ¼ cup shredded coconut, lightly toasted

Special Equipment
- Food processor
- Chinois or fine-mesh strainer
- 9-inch tart pan

Macadamia Haupia Tart

Haupia is a traditional Hawaiian dessert that, at its base, can be described as a luxurious and delicious pudding made with coconut milk. Since its creation, it has taken on many different forms. It's been known to double as a pie filling or to be paired with a chocolate ganache. Our version combines the classic coconut pudding with another beloved local ingredient: macadamia nuts. Store-bought gingersnaps and shortbread cookies fill out the crust, offering a hint of spice and extra buttery richness that perfectly complement both the macadamia nuts and the coconut filling.

To make the crust: Preheat the oven to 350°F.

In the bowl of a food processor, combine the shortbread cookies and gingersnaps. Pulse until they are a medium-fine texture, with some slightly larger chunks remaining. Add the macadamia nuts and salt and pulse until the texture of coarse sand. Transfer to a bowl and stir in the butter until the crumbs are completely coated.

Press the mixture into the bottom of a 9-inch tart pan. Use the bottom of a flat glass or measuring cup to press the crust uniformly along the bottom of the pan and firm the sides. Bake for 10 to 15 minutes, or until slightly darkened and set. Remove to a wire rack and let cool completely.

To make the filling: In a medium saucepan, whisk together the sugar and cornstarch until there are no clumps of cornstarch remaining. Whisk in the milk and coconut milk. Heat over medium heat. Cook the custard, whisking constantly, until it starts to bubble, 5 to 7 minutes; stop whisking every now and then, starting after 5 minutes, to check for bubbling.

Once the custard begins to bubble, set a 1-minute timer and whisk vigorously until it goes off. Remove the pan from the heat and strain through a chinois or fine-mesh strainer over a medium bowl. Whisk in the vanilla and coconut extract.

Pour the custard into the tart shell. Smooth it with a spatula and let cool to room temperature. Cover tightly with plastic wrap, pressing the wrap tight along the surface of the pudding, and refrigerate for at least 4 hours.

When ready to serve, sprinkle the shredded coconut over the top of the tart in an even layer. Refrigerate any leftover tart, tightly wrapped in plastic, for up to 3 days.

YIELD: SERVES 8 TO 12

TIME: 90 MINUTES, PLUS 3 HOURS COOLING

V

Cake
- 3 cups cake flour, sifted
- 2 cups finely shredded coconut
- 2 teaspoons baking powder
- 1¾ teaspoons kosher salt
- One 13.5-ounce can coconut milk
- 1 tablespoon fresh lime juice
- 1 cup unsalted butter, softened
- 1½ cups granulated sugar
- 2 teaspoons lime zest
- 4 large eggs, at room temperature
- 1 tablespoon pure vanilla extract
- 1 teaspoon coconut extract

Frosting
- 1 pound cream cheese, at room temperature
- 1 cup unsalted butter, at room temperature
- 2 cups powdered sugar
- ¼ cup cream of coconut
- ¼ teaspoon kosher salt
- 1 teaspoon pure vanilla extract
- ¼ teaspoon coconut extract

For Assembly
- ½ cup pineapple-passionfruit jam or pineapple jam
- 1½ cups coconut flakes, lightly toasted

Special Equipment
- Two 9-inch cake pans
- Stand mixer with paddle attachment

Coconut Cake

Here we offer a cake completely encased in toasted, flaky coconut—elegant, delicious, and a little bit of a mystery . . . just like many of our guests. We hate to spoil the surprise, but hidden among all that sweet coconut is a thin layer of pineapple jam that adds just the right amount of tartness to balance out the sweet. Coconut is, of course, a standout for discerning palates. You'll find it in various forms throughout: shredded coconut and coconut milk in the cake, cream of coconut and extract in the frosting, and the beautiful flakes on the outside.

To make the cake: Preheat the oven to 325°F. Grease two 9-inch cake pans and line the bottoms with parchment paper.

In a medium bowl, combine the cake flour, shredded coconut, baking powder, and salt. Whisk until completely combined. In a small bowl, whisk together the coconut milk and lime juice. If the coconut milk is separated, first put it in the blender and blend on high speed until uniform and smooth, 1 to 2 minutes.

In the bowl of a stand mixer fitted with a paddle attachment (or using a large bowl and a hand mixer), combine the butter, granulated sugar, and lime zest. Cream until pale and fluffy, 3 to 5 minutes. With the mixer running, add the eggs one at a time. Wait until each is fully incorporated before adding the next. Add the vanilla and coconut extract.

Decrease the speed to low and add about one-third of the flour mixture. Mix until just incorporated, then add half the coconut milk mixture. Beat until smooth. Repeat with the remaining dry and wet mixtures, finishing with the dry. Beat just until smooth.

Divide the batter evenly between the two pans. Bake for 30 to 35 minutes, or until a toothpick inserted into the center comes out with just a few moist crumbs clinging to it. Let the cakes cool in the pans for 10 minutes, then transfer to a wire cooling rack to cool completely.

To make the frosting: While the cakes cool, in the clean bowl of the stand mixer, cream together the cream cheese and butter on medium-high speed until light and creamy, 5 to 7 minutes. Stop and add the powdered sugar. Beat on low speed until moistened, then increase to medium-high and beat for 5 to 7 minutes more. Add the cream of coconut, salt, vanilla, and coconut extract. Beat until the frosting is smooth, creamy, and spreadable.

To assemble the cake: Use a long, serrated knife to level the tops of the cooled cakes. Save the scraps for snacks or cake pops. Peel off the parchment and place one of the cakes, cut-side up, on a platter. Spoon the pineapple jam on top and spread into a thin, even layer. Top with about one-third of the frosting and spread into an even layer.

Place the second cake, cut-side down, on top of the first. Spoon about one-third of the frosting on top and use an offset spatula to spread it in a thin layer all over the cake (called a "crumb coating," it keeps crumbs from marring the final frosted surface). Refrigerate the cake, uncovered, for 20 to 30 minutes, or until the frosting sets.

Frost the chilled cake with the remaining frosting, smoothed to an even layer all over. Carefully press handfuls of the toasted coconut flakes into the sides and top of the cake until evenly coated. Slice and serve. Leftover cake will keep for up to 4 days, tightly wrapped in plastic wrap and refrigerated.

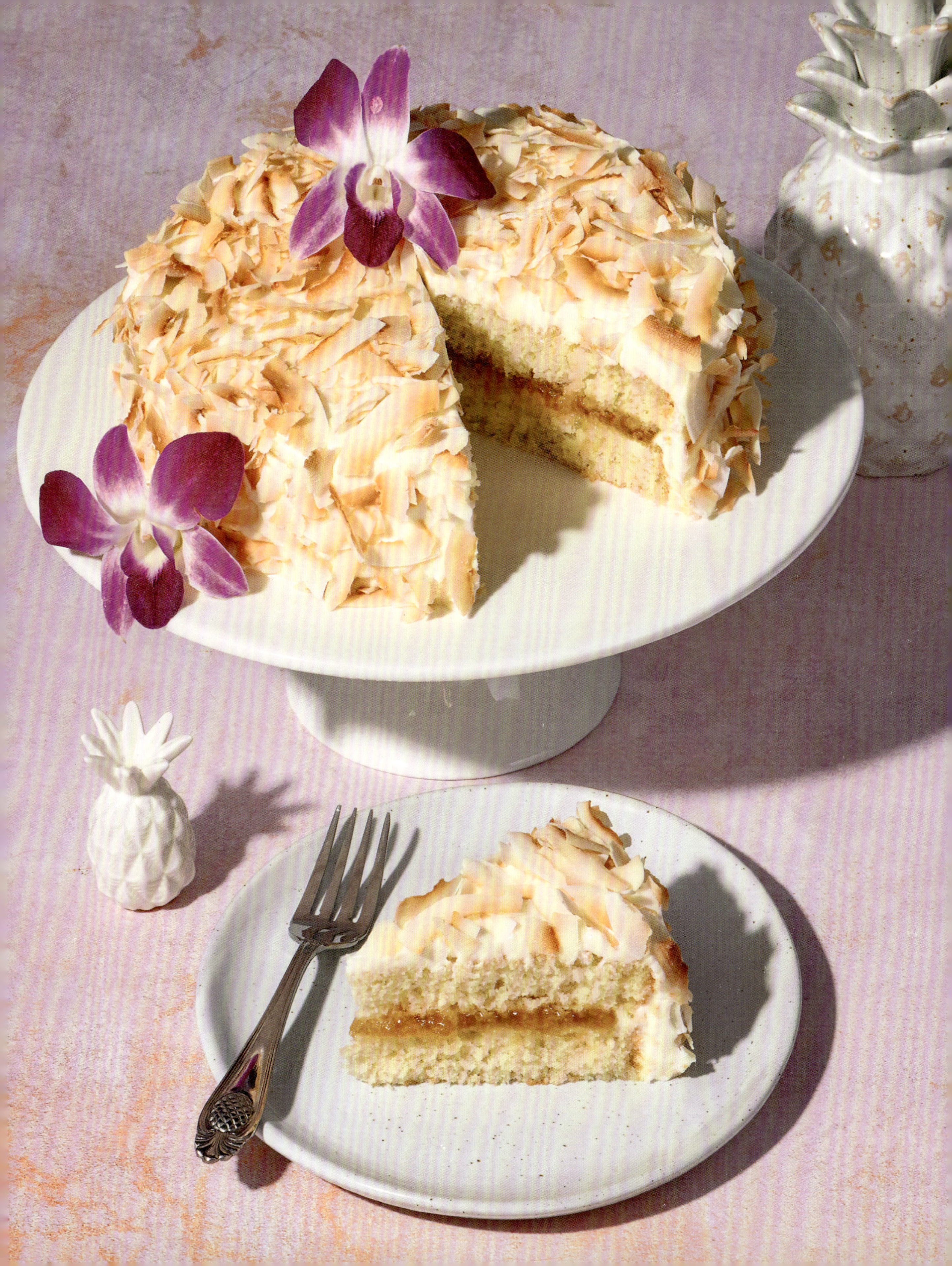

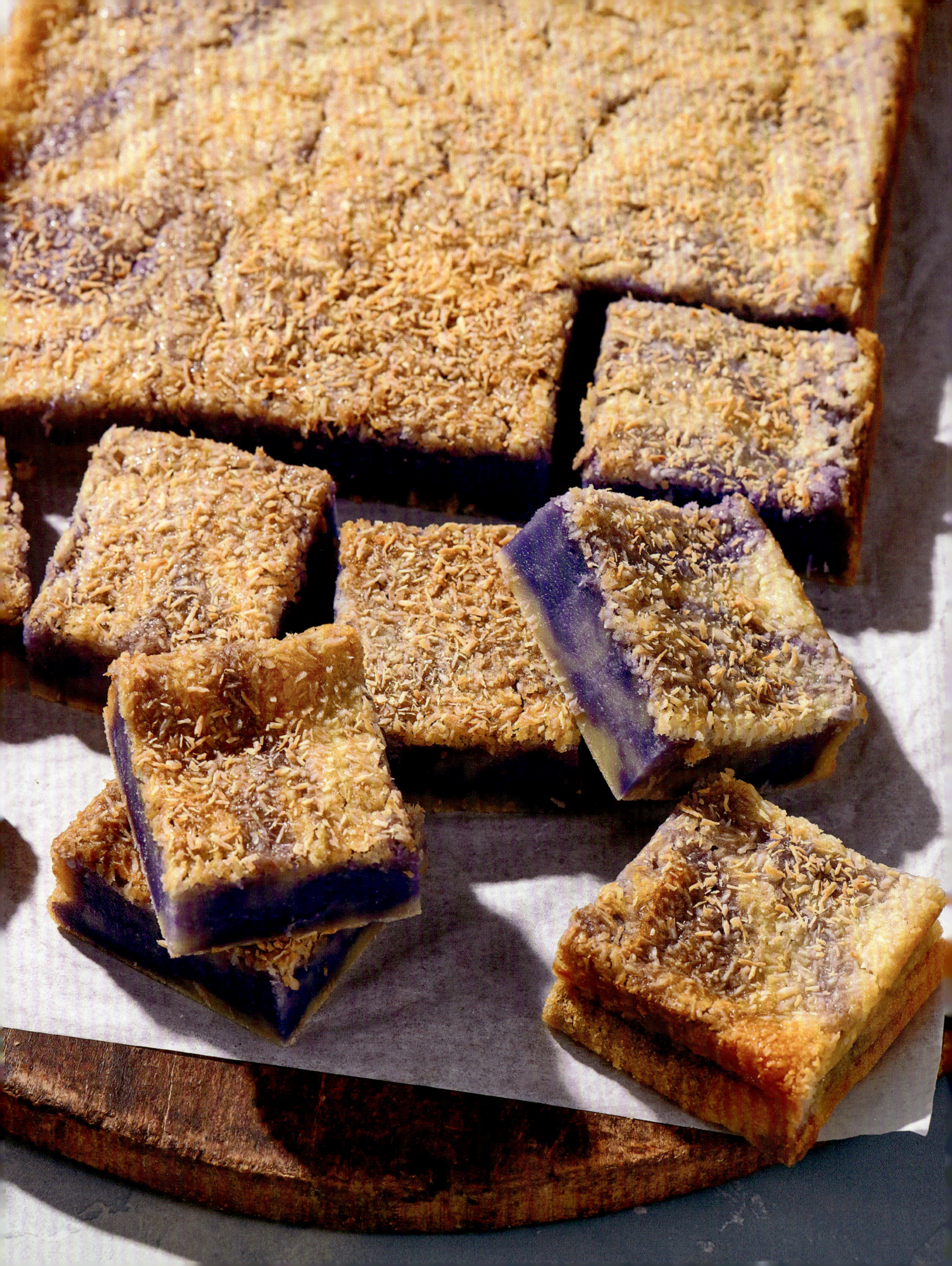

YIELD:
SERVES 12 TO 16
TIME:
90 MINUTES
GF, V

- 3 cups mochiko (sweet rice flour)
- 2 teaspoons baking powder
- ¾ teaspoon kosher salt
- 1½ cups sugar
- One 13.5-ounce can coconut milk
- 1½ cups whole milk, at room temperature
- 4 large eggs, at room temperature
- 6 tablespoons unsalted butter, melted and cooled
- 1 tablespoon pure vanilla extract
- ½ teaspoon ube extract
- ½ cup shredded coconut

Special Equipment
13-by-9-inch cake pan
Stand mixer with paddle attachment

Ube-Marbled Butter Mochi

Butter mochi is one of those desserts that evolves as it cools and chills, like taking a stroll around our grounds in the moonlight or even dozing off on the beach in the evening (though we'd ask that you exercise caution and leave any blankets, mattresses, or other equipment behind in your room). This dessert starts with a beautiful marbled effect, in which both plain and ube-flavored butter mochi are swirled together. Like many classic Hawaiian cakes, the top is covered with shredded coconut that is crispy and crunchy when it comes out of the oven. As the cake cools, usually by the next day, the coconut slowly absorbs moisture from the cake, turning soft and almost buttery. It's up to you which version you like best, though a tie is perfectly acceptable.

Preheat the oven to 350°F. Grease a 13-by-9-inch cake pan and line with parchment paper so that there's a 2-inch overhang on both long sides of the pan.

In the bowl of a stand mixer fitted with a paddle attachment, combine the mochiko, baking powder, salt, and sugar. Whisk until integrated.

Add the coconut milk (if the coconut milk has separated, blend it on medium-high speed until smooth and uniform before adding), whole milk, and eggs. Mix until smooth, with no lumps of mochiko remaining. Add the butter and vanilla, beating until just incorporated.

Pour three-quarters of the batter into the prepared pan. Add the ube extract to the remaining batter and mix until combined. Spoon dollops of the ube batter on top of the plain batter, then swirl a knife through the batter several times to create a marbled effect. Sprinkle the shredded coconut over the top in an even layer.

Bake until the cake is set and the coconut is golden brown, 65 to 75 minutes. Let cool completely in the pan before slicing and serving. Leftover cake will keep for up to 5 days, wrapped tightly with plastic wrap and refrigerated.

NOTE
Don't worry about overmixing this recipe. There isn't any gluten to overwork in the mochiko, so just mix as long as needed to hit those visual cues.

CHAPTER TWO
Sicily

At The White Lotus Resort & Spa in Sicily, we offer the very best *of* the best of this region of Italy. At the southernmost edge of the country, Sicilian agriculture is unique—the warmer climates aren't just great for sunbathing, swimming, and fishing on the beaches but also make for cuisine that differs from the rest of Italy. In Sicily, citrus truly sings in dishes like our Blood Orange and Fennel Salad (page 56), and Lemon Prosecco Granita (page 87). The deep blue waters surrounding the island host a variety of fish and shellfish, making them a quintessential element of the local cuisine. Of course, the region also has its signature pasta dishes, like Pasta con le Sarde (page 76), a meal that takes advantage of the abundance of top-quality sardines caught just off the coast. There's also Pasta alla Norma (page 74), which features delicious, meaty eggplants that thrive in the Mediterranean climate. If you've stayed with us before, you may remember that the iconic Cannoli (page 83), with its sweet, creamy ricotta filling, was actually invented in Sicily. The region has a rich history with an equally rich culinary scene—something we're proud to feature at our resort, along with top-notch service, stunning views, and a host of amenities and activities that are simply to *die* for.

MORNING SERVICE

Brioche col Tuppo

YIELD: MAKES 8
TIME: 75 MINUTES, PLUS 11 HOURS CHILLING AND RESTING
V

- ⅓ cup whole milk, lukewarm
- 2 tablespoons honey
- 3 cups bread flour
- ¼ cup sugar
- 1½ teaspoons kosher salt
- 1 tablespoon instant yeast
- 5 large eggs
- ¾ cup unsalted butter, softened
- 1 tablespoon water

Special Equipment
Stand mixer with dough hook attachment
Cooking thermometer

These charming brioche pastries are a classic Sicilian breakfast staple, something you'll remember from the buffet each morning. The *tuppo*, the small ball atop each roll, is a nod to one traditional way Sicilian women wore their hair: in a tight bun. While the hairstyle may fall in and out of fashion as the seasons pass—like so many things do—there is nothing unfashionable about a freshly baked brioche and a goblet of Coffee Granita (page 55) to start the morning. Sometimes a classic stays a classic for a reason.

In a large bowl, whisk the milk and honey until the honey dissolves. In the bowl of a stand mixer fitted with the dough hook attachment, combine the flour, sugar, salt, and yeast. Mix on low speed until combined. Add the milk mixture and mix until combined.

Add 4 of the eggs, one at a time. Mix until fully incorporated before adding the next. Increase the speed to medium and mix until a smooth dough forms, about 5 minutes.

Add the butter, 2 tablespoons at a time. Mix each addition until fully incorporated before adding more.

Mix the dough until smooth, shiny, and elastic, 10 to 15 minutes. The dough should pass the windowpane test. (Stretch a small portion of dough between your fingers and hold it up to a light source; you should be able to see light through it. If the dough doesn't tear, it's ready.) Transfer the dough to a greased, sealable container large enough to fit double the volume of dough. Refrigerate overnight, and up to 3 days.

When you're ready to make the brioche, let the dough sit out at room temperature for 2 hours. Line a half-sheet pan with parchment paper. Tip the dough out onto a clean work surface and divide it into 8 equal pieces. Pull a walnut-sized piece of dough from each.

Shape each large piece of dough by pulling it into a loose ball and tucking the sides under the bottom. Place the ball on the work surface and cup your hand over the ball, making a cage with your fingers. Turn your hand in a circle to tighten the ball of dough. Transfer the ball to the half-sheet pan.

Repeat with the remaining large dough balls. Then repeat the process with the small dough balls. Transfer them to the half-sheet pan as well. Cover the dough balls with greased plastic wrap and let rise for 45 to 60 minutes, or until noticeably puffy.

Preheat the oven to 375°F.

Press a divot into each of the large dough balls with your thumb. Place the small dough balls in the divots. In a small bowl, whisk the remaining egg with the water. Brush the egg wash all over the dough balls.

Bake for 25 to 30 minutes, or until golden brown and an instant-read thermometer registers at least 190°F when inserted into the center of a roll. Transfer to a wire rack to cool slightly. Serve warm with jam, butter, or Coffee Granita.

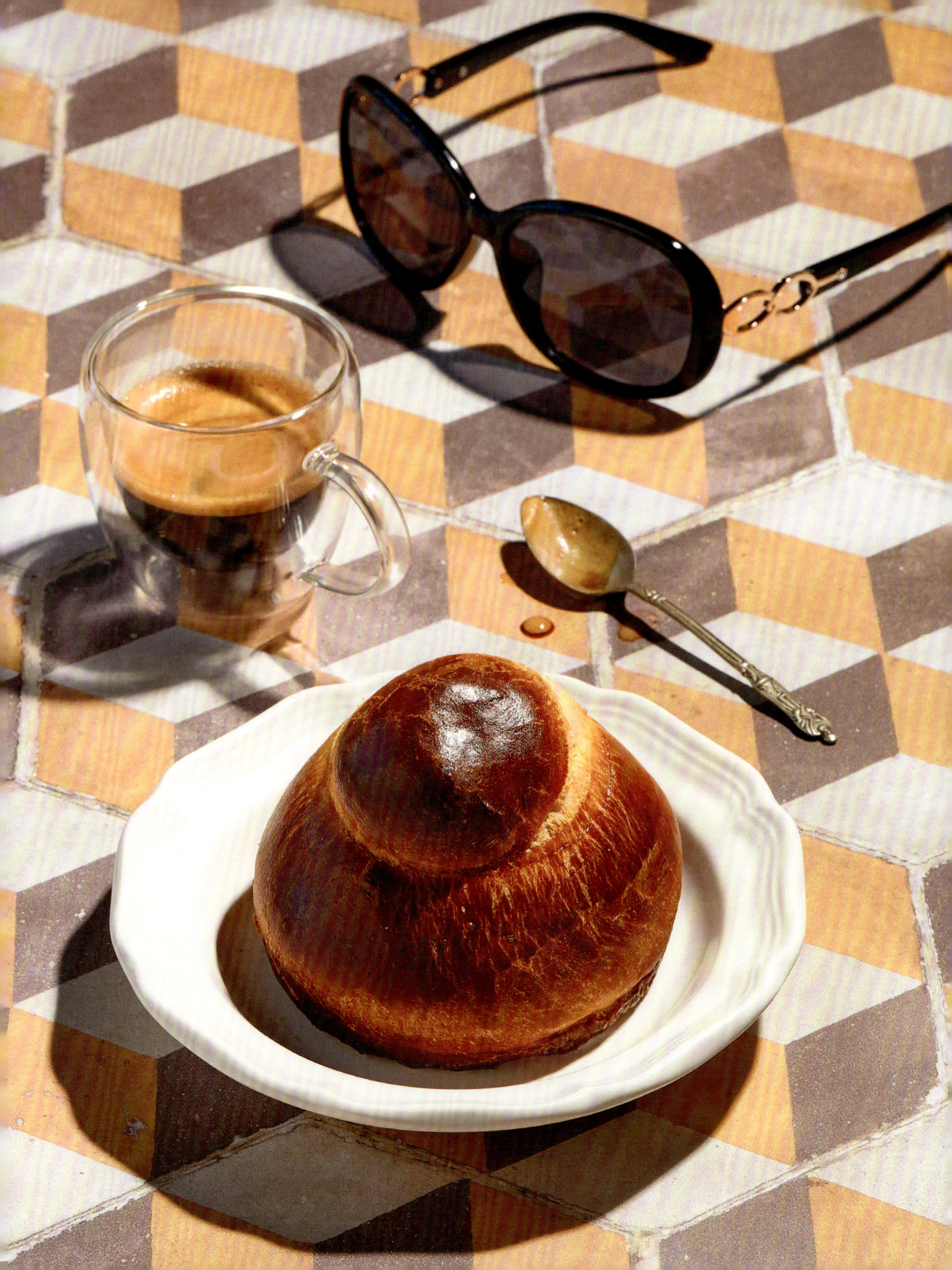

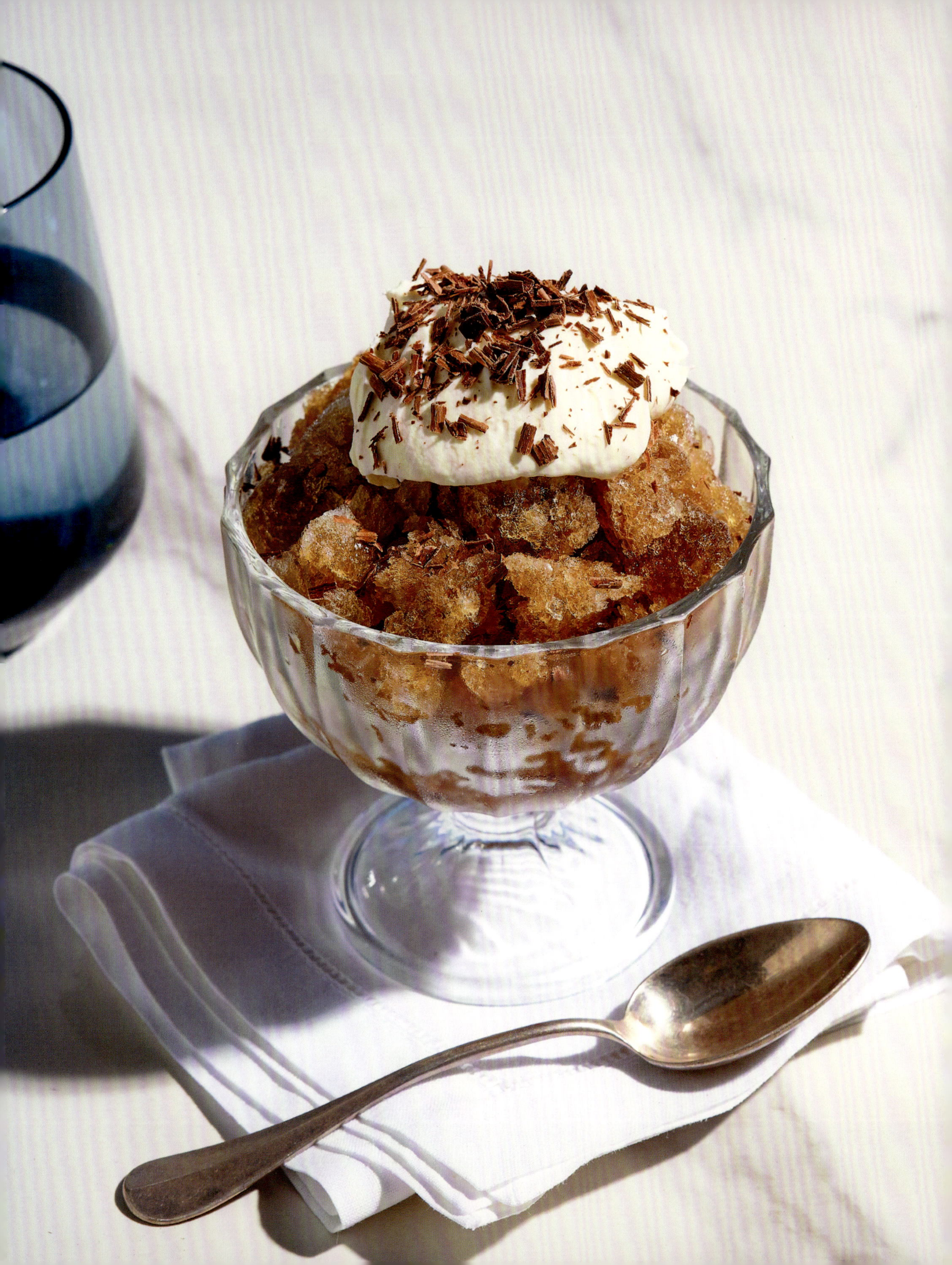

YIELD:
SERVES 6

TIME:
6 HOURS

GF, V

---

2 cups strong coffee or espresso, warm

⅓ cup raw sugar

¼ teaspoon kosher salt

1 teaspoon pure vanilla extract

For Assembly
1 cup heavy cream

1 tablespoon powdered sugar

Dark chocolate, for shaving

Special Equipment
2-quart freezer-safe container or metal baking pan

6 goblets or cocktail glasses

Coffee Granita

This semifrozen dessert should not be confused with *semifreddo* (Italian for "semifrozen"), which is a totally different dessert. Granita can be enjoyed any time, even in the morning. It's not uncommon to have a goblet of coffee granita alongside a warm Brioche col Tuppo (page 52) to start the day. Although you can use granulated sugar to make this dessert, we prefer the raw sugar with this recipe—it adds a little depth and some caramel notes that our guests seem to enjoy.

In a medium bowl, combine the coffee, raw sugar, and salt. Stir until the sugar and salt are dissolved. Stir in the vanilla. Pour into a 2-quart freezer-safe container or a metal baking pan.

Cover the pan and freeze for 30 minutes. Stir, breaking up any clumps of ice that have formed at the edges and corners of the container.

Repeat this process every 30 to 45 minutes for 6 hours, or until the mixture is completely frozen and no longer wet or slushy. It should resemble shaved ice. For the most appealing texture, eat the granita within a few days.

To assemble the granita: Whisk the cream and powdered sugar in a large bowl until soft peaks form, about 5 minutes. Divide the granita among six goblets or cocktail glasses. Top with the whipped cream and grate a small amount of dark chocolate over the top.

**YIELD:
SERVES 4
TIME:
15 MINUTES
GF, V**

- 1 large bulb fennel, stems trimmed
- 3 small blood oranges
- 1 tablespoon fresh lemon juice
- 2 tablespoons olive oil
- 1 tablespoon pistachio oil (optional) or more olive oil
- 1 teaspoon honey
- ¼ teaspoon kosher salt
- ¼ teaspoon black pepper
- ¼ cup roasted, salted pistachios, coarsely chopped

Blood Orange and Fennel Salad

This salad captures Sicilian produce at its best. Blood orange and fennel shine, while lemon juice, olive oil, pistachios, and pistachio oil all lend their support. It's a dish that seems simple at first glance when, in fact, it's full of complex flavors that dance on your palate the way waves crash onto the shore outside your suite during one of your stays with us. When you make this salad at home, our hope is that every bite evokes a beautiful memory of your time at The White Lotus.

Cut the fennel bulb in half, then cut the halves into thin slices. If you have a mandoline, use it to shave the fennel as thinly as possible. Otherwise, take your time with a good, sharp knife. Transfer to a mixing bowl.

Supreme the oranges. (Trim the top and bottom off the orange, so that it sits flat and the ends of the peel are exposed. Use a sharp knife to carefully cut off the peel, including the white pith. Then cut each individual orange segment from the membrane, so that only the flesh remains. Work over a bowl to catch the juice.) Transfer the oranges to the bowl with the fennel.

In a small bowl, combine the captured orange juice, lemon juice, olive oil, pistachio oil (if using), honey, salt, and pepper. Whisk until completely combined. Taste and adjust the seasoning as desired.

Pour the dressing over the fennel and oranges and toss to coat. Sprinkle with the pistachios and serve.

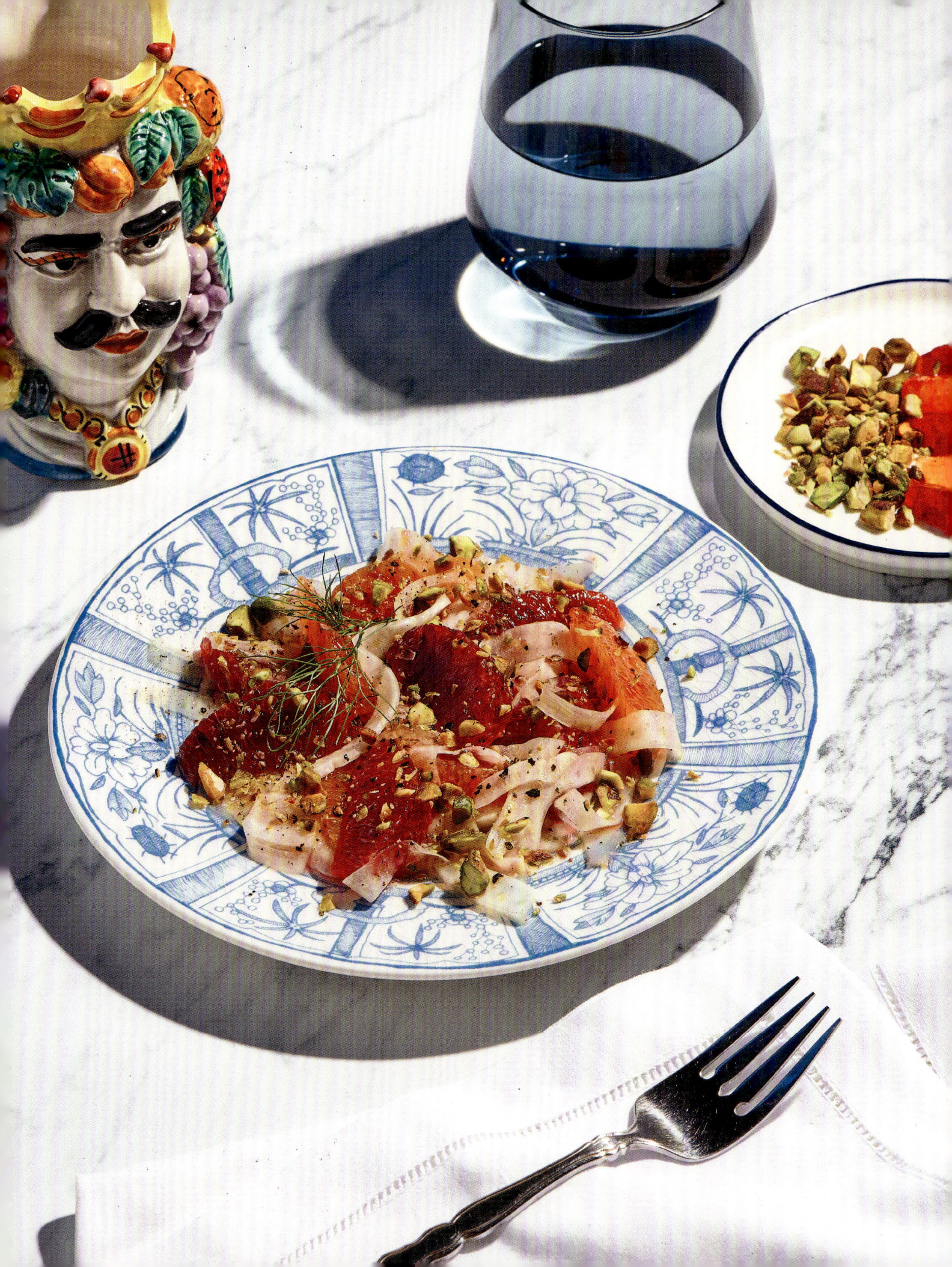

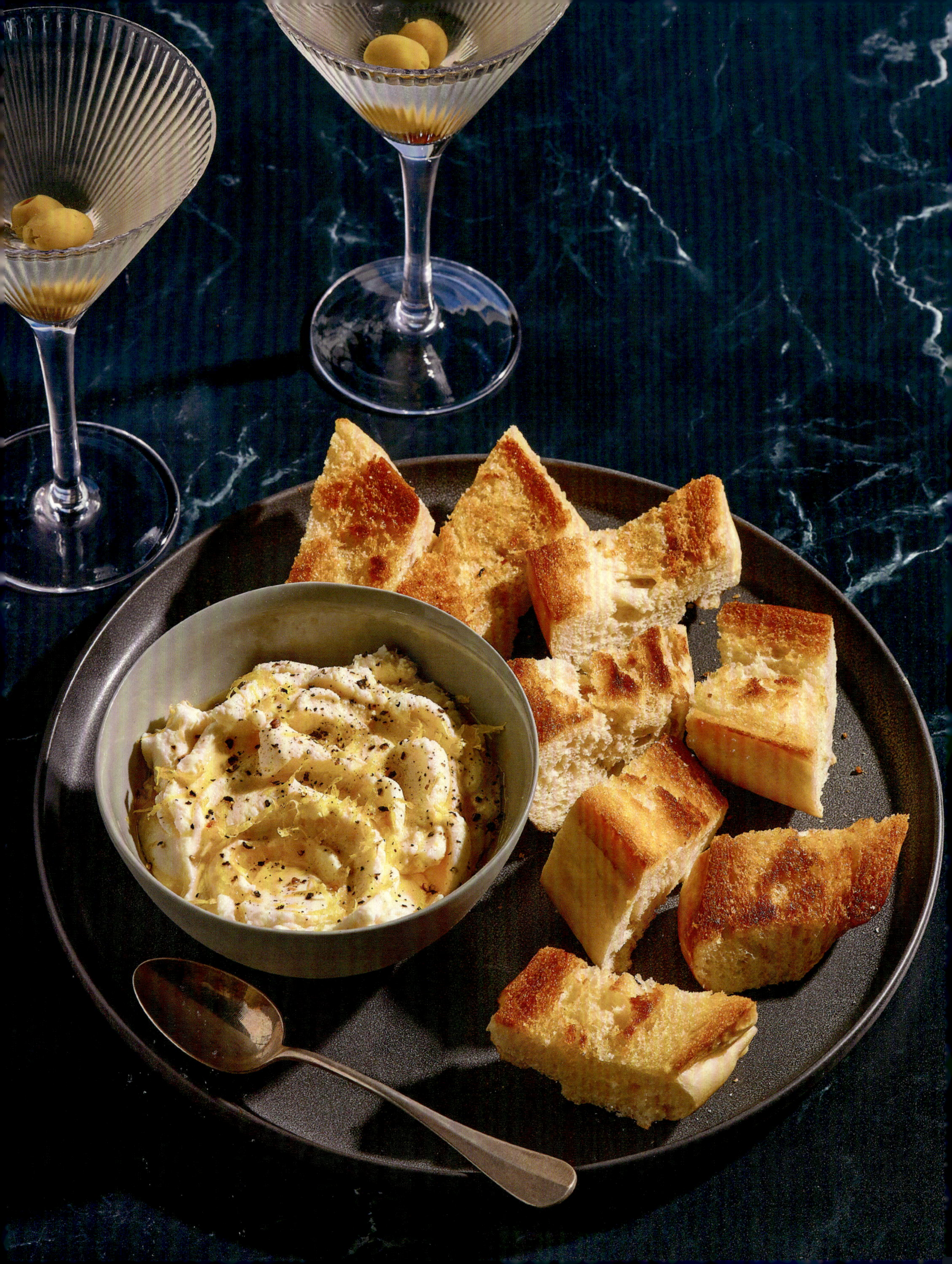

YIELD:
SERVES 4

TIME:
30 MINUTES

GF*, V

Ricotta
1 gallon whole milk
½ teaspoon kosher salt
¼ cup fresh lemon juice

For Serving
2 teaspoons olive oil
Flaky sea salt
Black pepper
Lemon zest
Crusty bread

Special Equipment
Cooking thermometer
Colander
Cheesecloth
Slotted spoon

Warm Ricotta with Lemon and Olive Oil

Those of you who participated in one of our tours will remember that ricotta is made from recooking the whey produced by making cheese. The word *ricotta* essentially means "cooked twice," after all. The version we serve on the property is made in this traditional way and sourced from local dairy farmers. However, we realize when you're cooking at home that you might not have that same level of access that we do, and we've adapted our recipe accordingly. Although this won't be exactly the same as the ricotta you've had here (then again, nothing is, is it?), we do think you'll find it quite tasty. This delicious starter is a favorite in our lounge, where you can listen to piano music from some very talented local performers.

To make the ricotta: In a large pot, combine the milk and salt. Gently bring to 180° to 190°F over medium-low heat, stirring occasionally. Once you reach the target temperature, stir in the lemon juice just until combined. Let sit over the heat, undisturbed, for 15 minutes—keep an eye on the temperature, adjusting the heat as needed to maintain 180° to 190°F. As the mixture heats, you'll notice curds start to separate and float to the top of the pot.

Check the temperature occasionally to make sure it's staying within the target range for the duration of cooking. While the mixture cooks, line a colander with four layers of cheesecloth, clipping the cloth to the edges of the colander. (You can place the colander over a bowl or directly in the sink.)

Transfer the curds from the pot to the lined colander with a slotted spoon. Let sit for 10 minutes to drain, then transfer to a serving bowl.

To serve: Drizzle with the olive oil, then sprinkle with flaky sea salt, freshly cracked black pepper, and lemon zest. Serve with crusty bread.

◆ NOTE ◆

The ricotta itself is gluten-free, but if you'd like to keep the recipe that way, serve on its own or replace the crusty bread with a gluten-free variety.

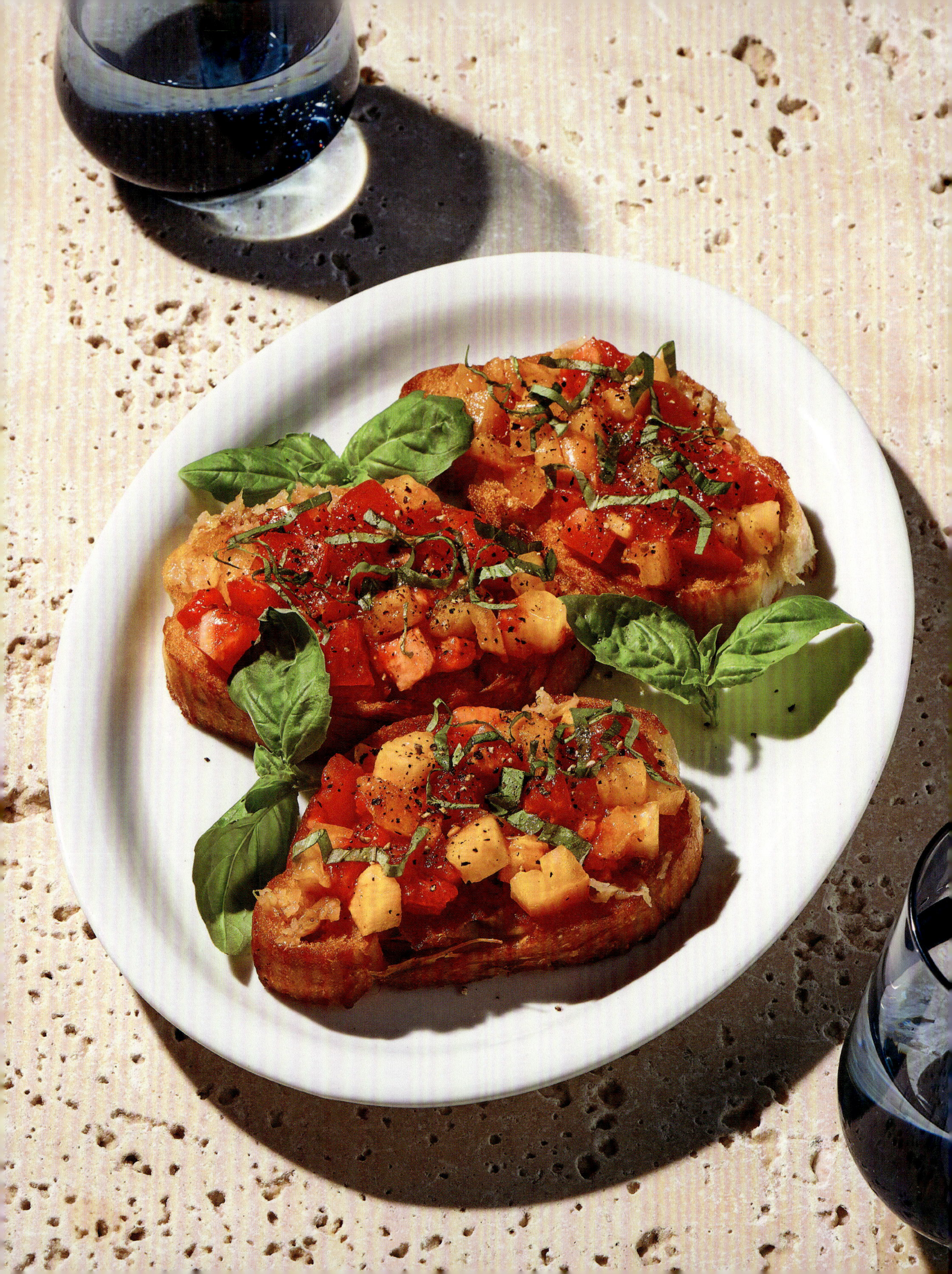

YIELD:
SERVES 4

TIME:
50 MINUTES

V

- ½ cup plus 1 tablespoon extra virgin olive oil
- 8 cloves garlic, peeled
- 4 slices Italian bread
- 1 pound heirloom tomatoes, diced
- 8 basil leaves
- 2 teaspoons balsamic vinegar
- Salt and pepper

Bruschetta

Bruschetta is a classic summery dish ideally made with ingredients at the peak of their season. A classic preparation you might recognize would start with grilled or toasted bread that's rubbed with a clove of garlic, then topped with fresh tomatoes, basil, and a bit of olive oil. As we like to do, we've added a little extra touch in the form of garlic confit. Preparing this first produces a garlic-infused oil that we brush onto fresh bread *before* toasting. Once these wonderful slices come out of the oven, we apply the sweet, fragrant confit before finally topping with tomatoes and basil. The garlic flavor becomes deeper and more complex, which our guests seem to love.

Preheat the oven to 400°F. Line a half-sheet pan with aluminum foil or parchment paper.

In a small saucepan, combine ½ cup of the olive oil and the garlic (the oil should completely cover the cloves; add more oil as needed). Cook over low heat until the garlic is light brown and soft, about 30 minutes. Remove the confit garlic from the heat and let cool.

Brush the now garlicky oil from the pan onto the bread slices and transfer them to the half-sheet pan. Bake until brown around the edges, 5 to 10 minutes.

Transfer the diced tomatoes to a medium bowl. Stack the basil leaves and roll them up in a tight coil. Thinly slice crosswise (this is called chiffonade). Add the basil to the bowl. Drizzle with the remaining 1 tablespoon olive oil and the balsamic vinegar. Season with a pinch of salt and black pepper and toss to coat.

Mash 1 to 2 tablespoons of the confit garlic onto each slice of toast. Top each with a quarter of the tomato mixture and serve immediately.

YIELD:
SERVES 4 TO 6

TIME:
35 MINUTES

GF, V (V+ IF SUBSTITUTING SUGAR FOR THE HONEY)

- 4 tablespoons extra virgin olive oil
- 1 small eggplant (about 1 pound), coarsely diced
- ¼ teaspoon salt
- 2 stalks celery, diced
- 1 small yellow onion, finely chopped
- 1 red bell pepper, cored and diced
- 4 cloves garlic, thinly sliced
- One 14-ounce can crushed tomatoes
- ¼ cup Sicilian olives, coarsely chopped
- 2 tablespoons capers, drained and rinsed
- 1 to 2 tablespoons honey or sugar
- 2 tablespoons balsamic vinegar
- 1 tablespoon sherry vinegar or more balsamic
- ½ cup pine nuts, toasted

Special Equipment
Dutch oven

Caponata

Caponata is a sweet-and-sour combination of fresh and brined vegetables that Sicily is known for: eggplant, tomatoes, olives, and so much more. The dish is extremely versatile: It can be enjoyed warm, at room temperature, or cold. It can be an appetizer served with bread, enjoyed on its own by the spoonful, or used on top of pasta. There are no wrong choices when it comes to caponata, except for letting it go to waste. That never seems to be a problem with this recipe!

In a Dutch oven over medium-high heat, heat 2 tablespoons of the olive oil until shimmering. Add the eggplant and salt. Cook until the eggplant has softened and is browning in spots, 5 to 8 minutes. Stir occasionally to prevent burning.

Add the remaining 2 tablespoons of olive oil to the Dutch oven. Stir in the celery, onion, and bell pepper. Cook until the onions are softened and translucent, about 5 minutes. Add the garlic and cook, stirring constantly, for 1 minute.

Add the tomatoes, olives, capers, 1 tablespoon of the honey, balsamic and sherry vinegars, and pine nuts. Decrease the heat to medium and cook, stirring occasionally, until the sauce is thickened and clinging to the vegetables, 10 to 15 minutes.

Adjust the seasonings to taste. Serve as you prefer—hot, at room temperature, or cold, on its own, as a side, or on pasta.

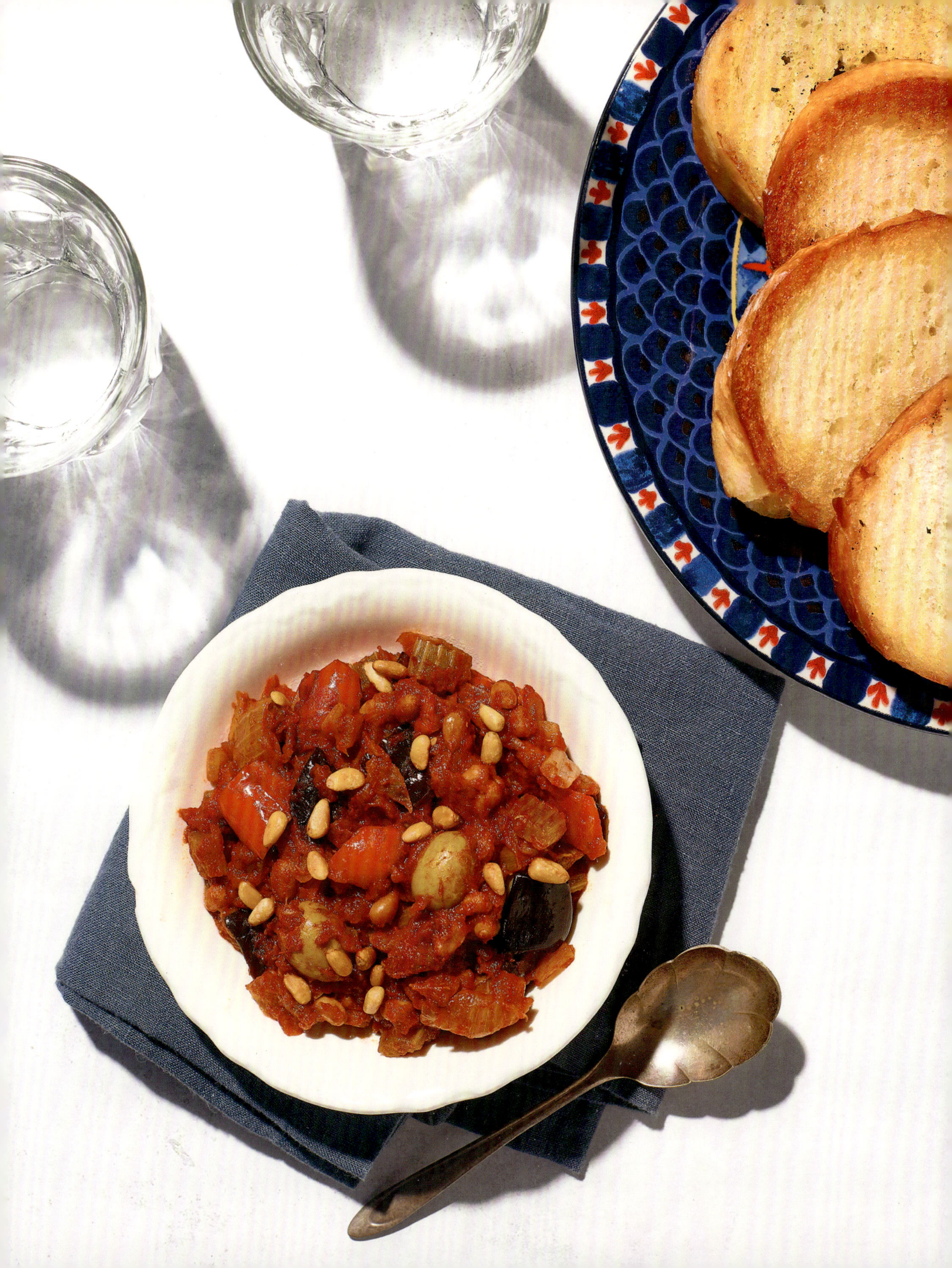

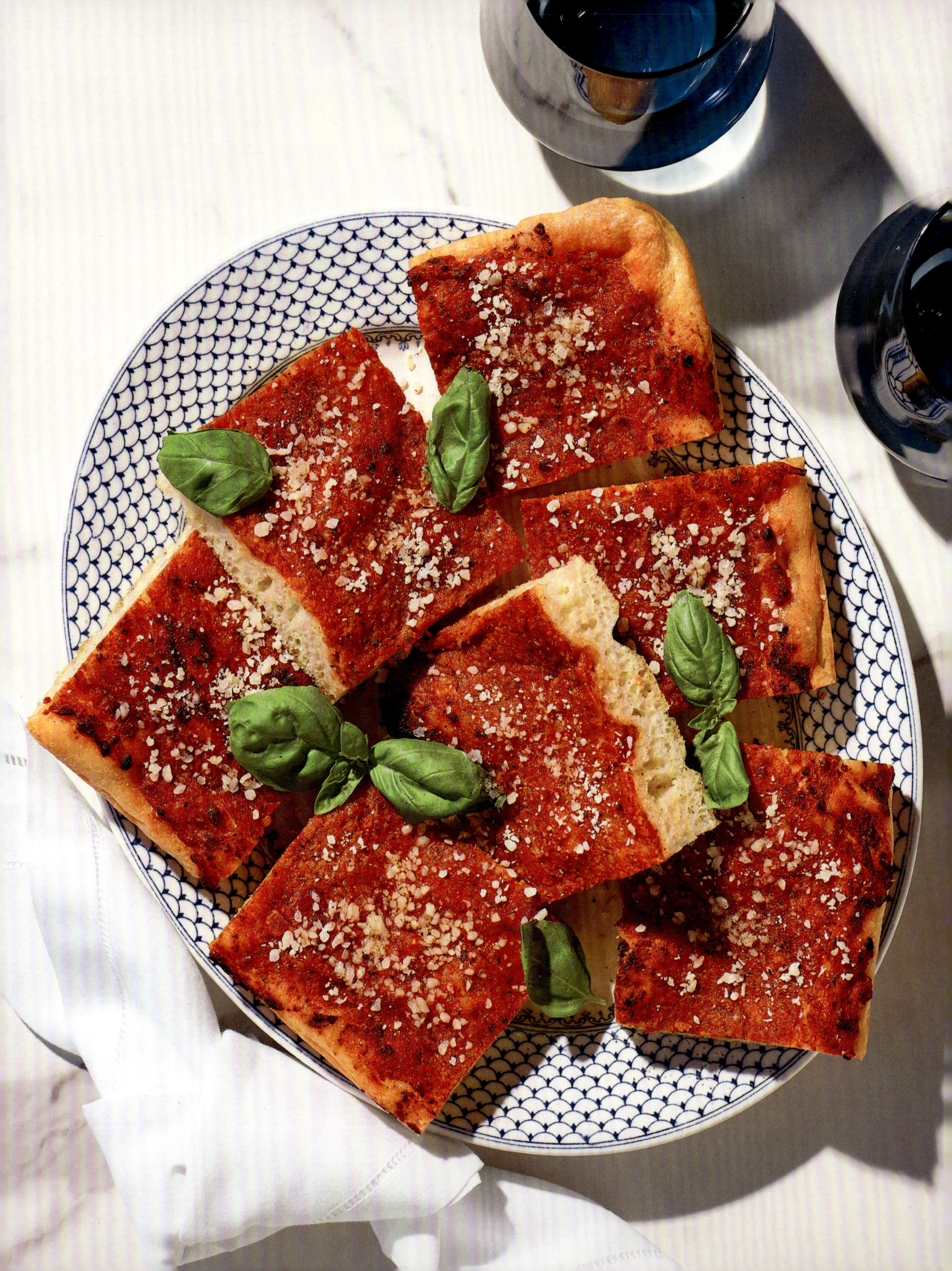

YIELD:
SERVES 4 TO 6

TIME:
30 MINUTES, PLUS UP TO 3 DAYS RESTING

Dough
3½ cups 00 flour
½ cup semolina
1½ teaspoons instant yeast
2 teaspoons kosher salt
½ cup olive oil
1½ cups lukewarm water

Sauce
2 tablespoons extra virgin olive oil
1 medium yellow onion, thinly sliced
2 cups passata (tomato purée)
4 anchovies, finely chopped
1 cup breadcrumbs
1½ cups grated caciocavallo or Pecorino Romano

Special Equipment
Stand mixer with dough hook attachment
Dutch oven

Sfincione

Pizza can take many forms in Italy, from the thin-crusted regional favorite of Napoli to the thick-crusted one beloved in Sicily. Each city has its own variation. Our recipe is a fairly classic preparation, with a tomato sauce thickened with breadcrumbs, along with cheese, anchovies, and caramelized onions. Unlike other pizza variations, the cheese is mixed into the sauce here. And it is typically a stronger aged cheese, such as caciocavallo. If you can't find that stateside, Pecorino Romano is a perfectly good substitute. If you're looking to make new friends, this recipe is sure to impress—but be confident in the company you've chosen before you step into the kitchen, or onto somebody's boat . . .

To make the dough: In the bowl of a stand mixer fitted with the dough hook attachment, combine the flour, semolina, yeast, and salt. Mix on low speed for about 1 minute, just until the ingredients are combined. With the mixer running, add 3 tablespoons of the olive oil and the water. Continue mixing until a shaggy dough forms. Increase the speed to medium and mix for 10 to 15 minutes, or until the dough is smooth, shiny, and elastic.

Grease a bowl or sealable container with 1 tablespoon of olive oil. Transfer the dough to the container. Cover and refrigerate for 24 hours, and up to 3 days.

Grease a half-sheet pan with the remaining ¼ cup of olive oil. Transfer the dough to the prepared pan. Roll it to coat with oil, then wrap it in plastic wrap or cover with an inverted half-sheet pan. Let it rise for 2 to 3 hours, or until quite puffy and doubled in volume.

To make the sauce: In a Dutch oven over medium-high heat, heat the olive oil until shimmering. Add the onion and cook, stirring occasionally, until softened and brown at the edges, 5 to 7 minutes. Add a splash of water and decrease the heat to medium. Continue cooking for 20 to 30 minutes, adding small amounts of water whenever the pan goes dry. The onions should be quite soft and beginning to caramelize.

Stir in the passata, anchovies, breadcrumbs, and cheese. Remove the pan from the heat and let cool while the dough continues to rise.

Place a rack in the lower position and preheat the oven to 450°F.

Gently spread the dough, lifting and pulling, until it completely fills the pan. Cover and let rise again until puffy, about 15 to 30 minutes.

Spread the sauce over the dough, being careful not to deflate the dough too much (it will deflate a little—that's totally normal).

Bake for 25 to 30 minutes, until the crust is golden brown. Lift the crust up with a thin, flat spatula to check the bottom—it's important that the bottom is also golden brown and crisp. Let cool in the pan for 5 to 10 minutes before slicing and serving hot.

YIELD:
MAKES 8

TIME:
3 HOURS

Ragù
2 tablespoons extra virgin olive oil

1 large carrot, peeled and diced

2 stalks celery, diced

1 medium yellow onion, diced

½ teaspoon kosher salt, plus a pinch

¼ teaspoon black pepper, plus a pinch

6 cloves garlic, minced

Pinch of red pepper flakes

8 ounces ground pork

8 ounces ground beef

1 cup red wine

One 28-ounce can plum tomatoes

Rice
4 cups water

½ teaspoon kosher salt

1 cup carnaroli or Arborio rice

3 tablespoons unsalted butter

¼ cup grated Parmesan or pecorino cheese

For Assembly
4 ounces mozzarella or Scamorza, cut into 8 cubes

⅓ cup all-purpose flour

1 cup water

1 cup breadcrumbs

2 quarts vegetable or other neutral oil

Special Equipment
6-quart (or larger) Dutch oven

Arancini

At first glance, you might mistake a well-made arancini for a small orange. That is, after all, where the name comes from—the Italian word for "little oranges." They are not little oranges (although Sicily is known for its unparalleled citrus), but rather balls of rice packed with any number of fillings. We like one of the more traditional preparations, which incorporates a delicious classic ragù and cheese. Although we hear it's common stateside to make arancini from leftover risotto, we find it *uncommon* for there be any leftover risotto at all when we make it here. If you are starting from scratch, we consider carnaroli to be an ideal rice, but Arborio is also a strong option.

To make the ragù: In a large Dutch oven over medium-high heat, heat the olive oil until shimmering. Add the carrot, celery, and onion and season with a healthy pinch of salt and black pepper. Cook, stirring occasionally, until the vegetables are softened and the onions turn translucent, 7 to 10 minutes. Add the garlic and red pepper flakes and cook, stirring constantly, for 1 minute.

Add the ground pork and beef. Season with the remaining ½ teaspoon kosher salt and ¼ teaspoon black pepper. Break the meat apart with a wooden spoon until it's cooked through, 5 to 7 minutes. Add the wine and stir. Cook until it is almost completely evaporated, 3 to 5 minutes. Add the tomatoes and crush them with a potato masher.

Bring the sauce to a boil, then decrease to a simmer. Simmer the ragù, stirring occasionally, until it is reduced and quite thick, 20 to 30 minutes. Taste and season as needed. Remove from the heat and let cool. (You can make the ragù up to 5 days ahead. Store refrigerated in a sealed container.)

To make the rice: In a large saucepan over high heat, combine the water and salt and bring to a boil. Stir in the rice, return to a boil, then decrease to a simmer. Cover and cook for 18 to 22 minutes, or until all of the water has evaporated. Stir in the butter and Parmesan, mixing until creamy. Cover and let cool to room temperature.

To assemble the arancini: Divide the rice into 8 equal portions. Place two-thirds of a portion in the palm of your hand and flatten it into a thin patty. Top with a scoop of ragù and one mozzarella cube. Ball the patty around the ragù and cheese and top with the remaining one-third of the portion. Gently seal the rice around the filling. Transfer to a plate and repeat with the remaining rice, ragù, and cheese. Refrigerate the arancini while you prepare the breading and oil.

In a small bowl, whisk the flour and water, adjusting with more of one or the other until it is the consistency of heavy cream. Transfer to a wide, shallow bowl. Add the breadcrumbs to a separate wide, shallow bowl.

Continued on page 68.

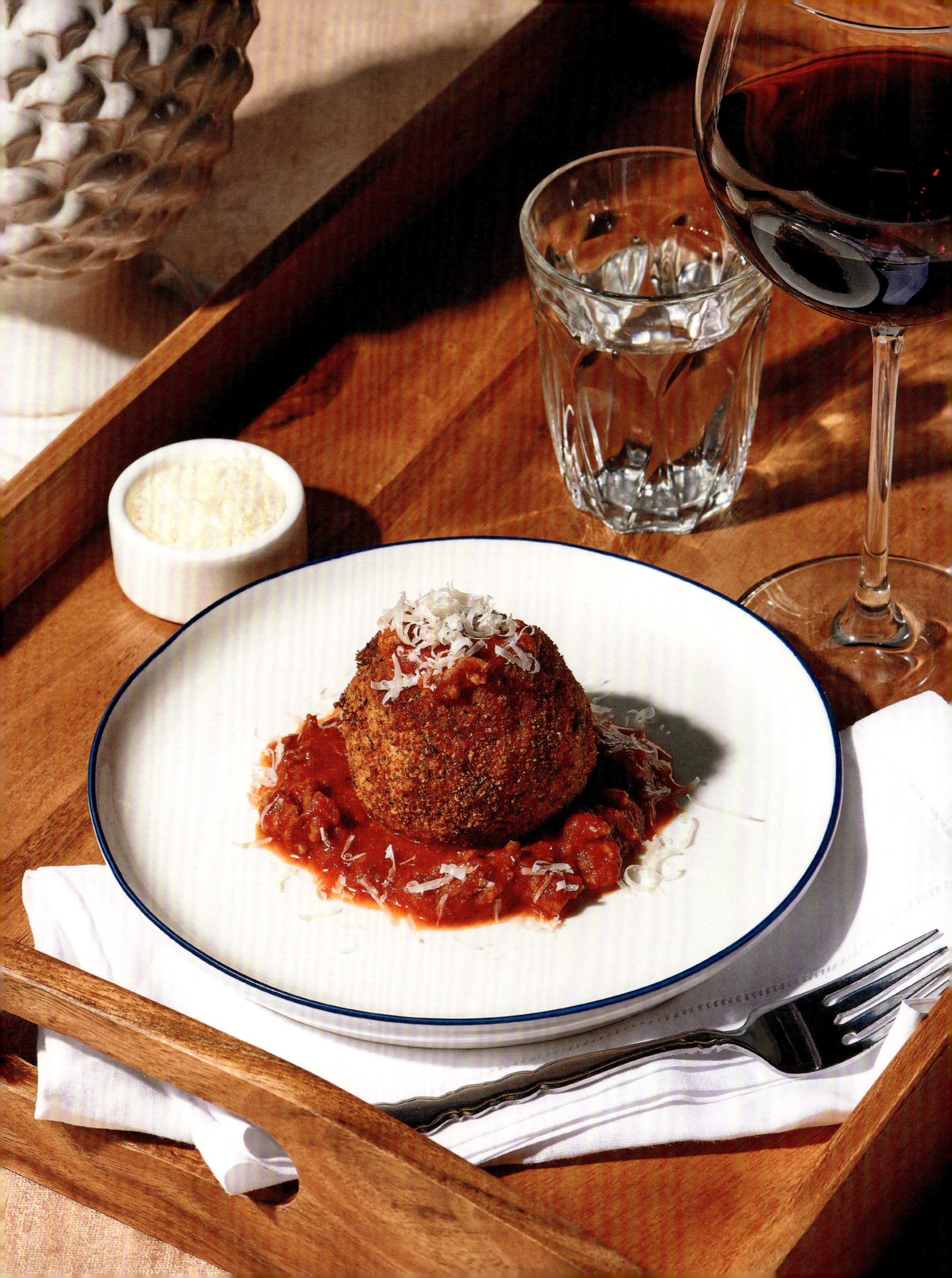

Arancini Continued

In a 6-quart or larger Dutch oven, heat the oil over medium-high heat until it reaches 375°F. Adjust the heat as necessary to maintain that temperature. Line a half-sheet pan with aluminum foil and set a wire rack in the pan.

Working one at a time, dip the arancini into the flour mixture and allow the excess to drip off. Roll the ball in the breadcrumbs and return to the plate.

Working in batches, fry the arancini for 5 to 8 minutes, until deeply golden brown (if the oil doesn't completely cover the arancini, flip them about halfway through). Remove the arancini with a wire skimmer and transfer to the wire rack.

Repeat with the remaining arancini. Serve hot, with warm ragù on the side, if desired. Leftover arancini can be reheated in a 400°F oven for 10 to 15 minutes, or until warmed through. Refrigerate leftovers in a sealed container for up to 5 days.

NOTE

A good rule of thumb when frying is to only take up half the surface area of the oil with whatever you're frying. Crowding the pot can lower the oil temperature and lead fried food to absorbing too much grease.

YIELD:
SERVES 4

TIME:
45 MINUTES

- 3 tablespoons extra virgin olive oil
- 1 small yellow onion, finely chopped
- 4 cloves garlic, minced
- ¼ teaspoon red pepper flakes
- 1 cup dry white wine
- 1 pound mussels, well-scrubbed, beards removed
- ½ teaspoon kosher salt, plus more for cooking pasta
- 1 pound bucatini
- 1 cup fish, seafood, or lobster stock
- 2 cups passata (tomato purée)
- ¼ teaspoon black pepper
- 8 ounces sea scallops
- 16 large shrimp
- 1 pound steamed lobster meat
- ¼ cup unsalted butter, cubed

Special Equipment
Dutch oven

EVENING SERVICE

Pasta Pescatore

Celebrate the gorgeous coast with this pasta dish. More than a few guests have called it "utterly decadent." You'll find the fulsome bucatini positively swims in this sauce, made by combining tomato sauce with fish stock. Our Pasta Pescatore is studded with mussels, shrimp, scallops, and succulent lobster meat. However, you needn't be constrained by this list of seafood when you prepare your own. Like so many restaurants around here, ours included, this pasta dish is meant to showcase the freshest catches of the day, whatever they may be. The richness of this dish makes it perfect for celebrating special occasions, like a financial windfall, for instance.

In a Dutch oven over medium-high heat, heat the oil until shimmering. Add the onion and cook, stirring frequently, until softened and translucent, 5 to 7 minutes. Add the garlic and red pepper flakes and cook, stirring constantly, for 1 minute.

Add the wine and bring to a boil (this should happen almost instantly). Add the mussels. Cover and cook until all the mussels have opened, about 5 minutes. Use a slotted spoon or wire skimmer to transfer the cooked mussels to a bowl. Let cool until safe to handle.

Meanwhile, bring a large pot of salted water to a boil over high heat. Add the bucatini, which should finish cooking around the same time as the sauce is finished.

While the mussels cool, heat the leftover cooking liquid in the Dutch oven over medium-high heat. Add the fish stock and passata. Season with the ½ teaspoon of salt and the pepper. Bring to a boil, then decrease the heat to medium. Cook, stirring frequently, until slightly reduced and thickened, about 10 minutes.

Add the scallops and shrimp. Cook, stirring frequently, until just cooked through, 3 to 5 minutes. Add the lobster meat and cook just until warmed through, 2 to 3 minutes longer. Stir in the butter until melted and the sauce is emulsified. Remove the Dutch oven from the heat.

Remove the mussels from their shells and add them to the sauce. Once the pasta is done cooking (consult the package directions for exact timing, and cook to al dente), drain, reserving about 1 cup of the cooking liquid. Transfer the pasta to the sauce, along with ½ cup of the pasta water. Toss and stir until the pasta is completely coated.

Divide the pasta among four bowls. Divide the seafood evenly among each bowl. Serve hot.

YIELD:
SERVES 4 TO 6

TIME:
1 HOUR

GF, V+

2 tablespoons olive oil, plus more for spatula
2 cups water
¾ teaspoon kosher salt
1 cup chickpea flour
½ teaspoon black pepper
2 tablespoons minced fresh parsley
2 quarts vegetable or other neutral oil

For Serving
Flaky sea salt
Lemon wedges

Special Equipment
Dutch oven
Cooking thermometer

Panelle

You may have seen street vendors selling these crispy, crunchy fritters on your walking food tour of the city—one of the more popular activities available through the concierge. Many vendors sell panelle in sandwiches. We agree that they make a wonderful filling for a seeded roll. However, we love to serve them on their own, with just a squeeze of lemon. After all, simple can be elegant, and that's an ethos we believe our guests have come to expect from us.

Spread the olive oil on a half-sheet pan.

In a large pot, combine the water, salt, and chickpea flour, whisking until smooth. Place the pot over medium-high heat and continue whisking until the mixture is thick like polenta, 4 to 6 minutes. The panelle batter is ready once it starts to pull away from the sides of the pot. Stir in the black pepper and parsley and remove from the heat.

Pour the batter onto the half-sheet pan and spread into a layer about ⅛ inch thick. (Use a greased offset spatula to spread the batter.) Cover the pan with plastic wrap and let cool to room temperature. The batter will firm up quite a bit.

In a Dutch oven over medium to medium-high heat, heat the vegetable oil to 375°F. Line a second half-sheet pan with aluminum foil and set a wire rack over the foil. While the oil heats, cut the cooled batter into 2-by-2-inch squares.

When the oil reaches temperature, add a few of the panelle squares. Don't crowd the oil (see Note, page 68). Fry the panelle for 3 to 4 minutes, or until golden. Flip and fry for 3 to 4 minutes more. Use a wire skimmer to transfer the cooked panelle to the cooling rack. Sprinkle with a pinch of flaky salt. Repeat with the remaining batter, and serve the panelle hot, with lemon wedges.

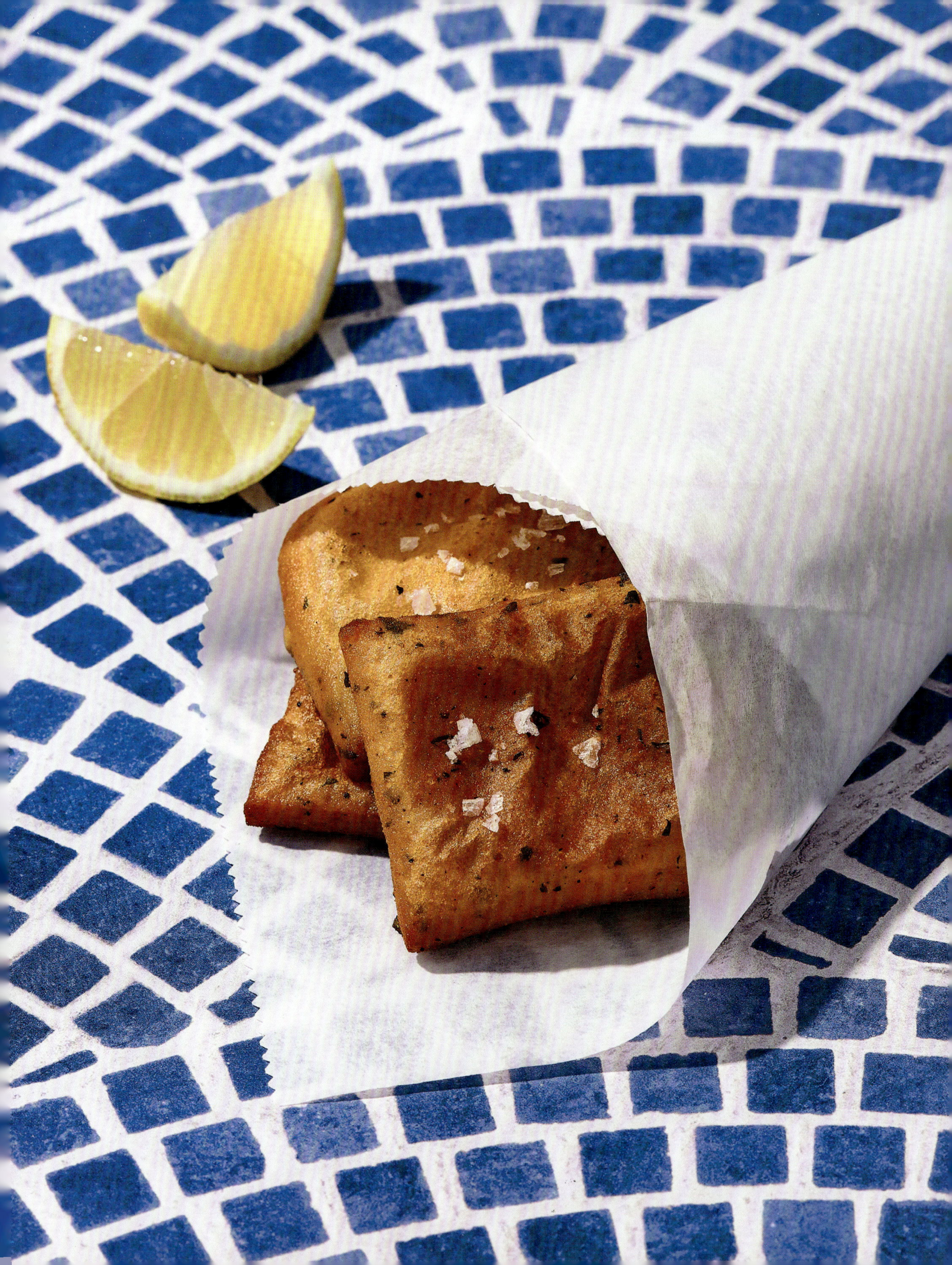

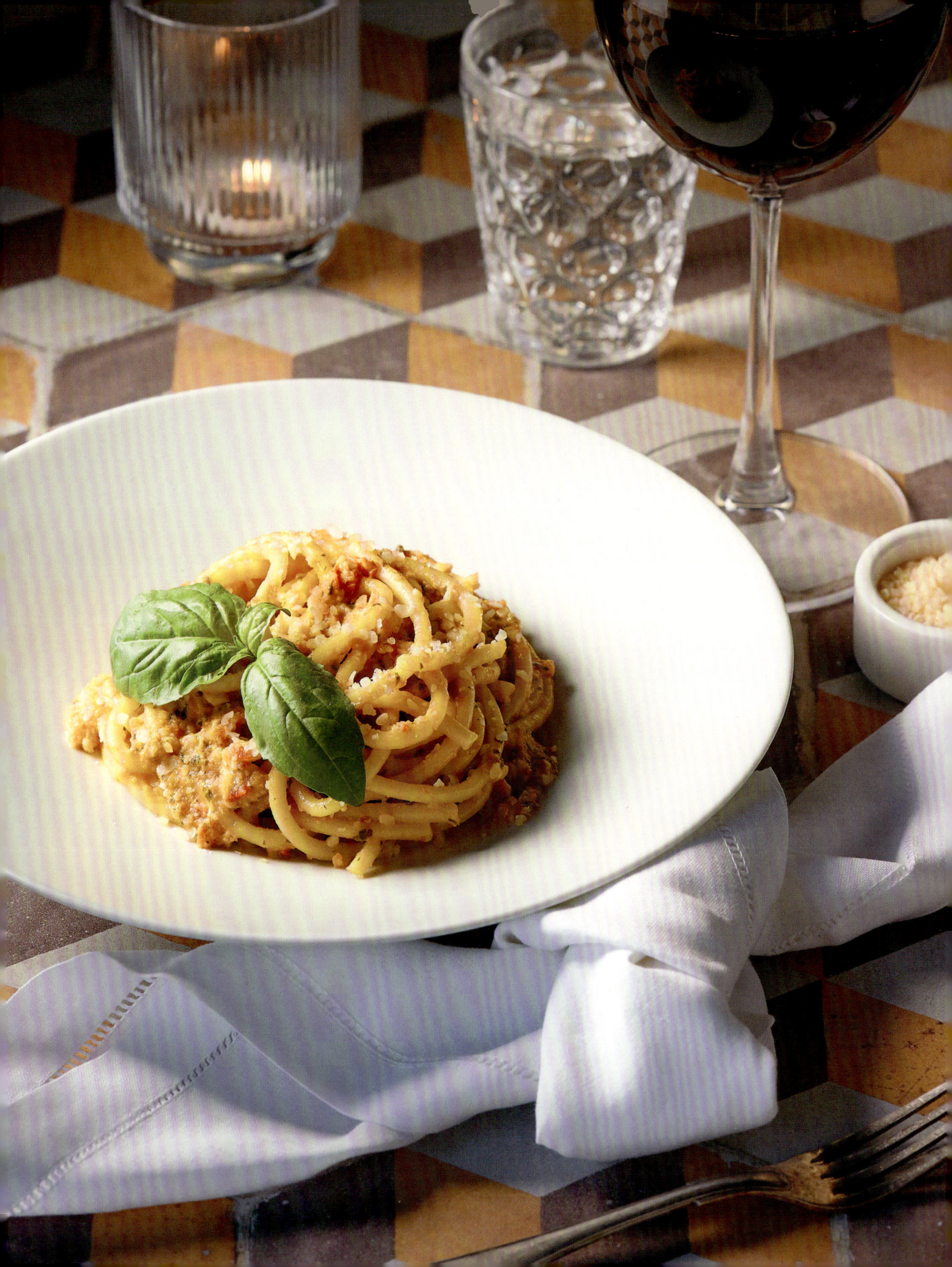

YIELD:
SERVES 4 TO 6
TIME:
45 MINUTES
V

- ½ cup blanched almonds
- 2 cloves garlic, peeled
- 30 fresh basil leaves
- 4 Roma tomatoes, seeded and coarsely chopped
- ¼ cup grated Pecorino Romano cheese, plus more to serve
- ¼ cup extra virgin olive oil
- Salt
- 1 pound long pasta, such as spaghetti, linguini, or bucatini

Special Equipment
Food processor

Pasta con Pesto alla Trapanese

Many of our guests are familiar with the famous pesto from Genoa—it has become rather popular, it seems. But we enjoy this local variation, which uses tomatoes and toasted almonds along with the usual suspects: basil, garlic, cheese, and olive oil. The result is a pesto that's slightly tangy and fruity with a deep, nutty flavor.

Preheat the oven to 350°F.

Spread the almonds on a quarter-sheet pan. Toast them until dark and fragrantly nutty, about 10 minutes. Let cool completely.

Add the almonds and garlic to a food processor and pulse until coarsely chopped. (Don't be tempted to blitz them fine; they'll be broken down during cooking with the other ingredients.) Add the basil, tomatoes, cheese, and oil. Pulse until a thick paste forms. It should be slightly coarse with some texture, although all the ingredients should be uniform and blended.

Bring a large pot of salted water to a boil over high heat. Cook the pasta according to the package instructions. Drain, reserving at least 1 cup of the pasta water. Return the pasta to the pot. Add the pesto. Toss to combine, then add ½ cup of the pasta water, stirring and tossing until emulsified. Add more water as necessary for a thick sauce that clings to the pasta.

Divide the pasta among bowls, topping with any remaining pesto and additional cheese. Serve hot.

YIELD:
SERVES 4

TIME:
30 MINUTES

V

- 2 medium eggplant, cubed
- 6 tablespoons extra virgin olive oil
- 1 teaspoon kosher salt, plus more for cooking pasta
- ¼ teaspoon black pepper
- 3 cloves garlic, finely chopped
- ¼ teaspoon red pepper flakes
- One 28-ounce can whole plum tomatoes
- 1 pound penne pasta
- 4 ounces ricotta salata, grated

Special Equipment
Dutch oven

Pasta alla Norma

This Sicilian specialty is a celebration of robust flavors. Roasted or fried eggplant introduces a smoky complexity to an otherwise simple tomato sauce, while a pile of shredded ricotta salata brings a salty balance to the dish. Historically, preparation involves pan-frying slices of eggplant in batches—a lengthy process. However, we understand our guests expect a certain, more relaxed approach from time to time. That's why this recipe is designed so you can roast the eggplant all at once, while you prepare the tomato sauce. It makes for a quick meal, but not at the expense of that luxurious taste. It also happens to serve four people, making it an ideal way to impress that other couple on your next double date.

Preheat the oven to 450°F. Line a half-sheet pan with parchment paper.

Place the eggplant in a large bowl. Drizzle with 4 tablespoons of the olive oil and sprinkle with ½ teaspoon of the kosher salt and the black pepper. Toss to coat. Transfer to the sheet pan, spreading it out in an even layer, and roast for 20 minutes, or until softened and beginning to brown in some spots.

Meanwhile, in a Dutch oven over medium-high heat, heat the remaining 2 tablespoons of oil until shimmering. Add the garlic and red pepper flakes and stir constantly for 1 minute. Add the tomatoes and the remaining ½ teaspoon of kosher salt.

Smash the tomatoes with a potato masher. Bring the sauce to a boil, then decrease to a simmer. Add the eggplant to the sauce, stirring it in. Taste and adjust the seasonings as needed. Simmer the sauce, stirring occasionally, while you prepare the pasta.

Bring a large pot of salted water to a boil over high heat. Cook the pasta according to the package instructions. Drain, reserving about 1 cup of the pasta water. Add the pasta to the sauce, along with ½ cup of the pasta water. Stir to combine, adding more pasta water if needed to achieve the desired thickness.

Divide the pasta among four bowls. Top each with an equal amount of ricotta salata and serve.

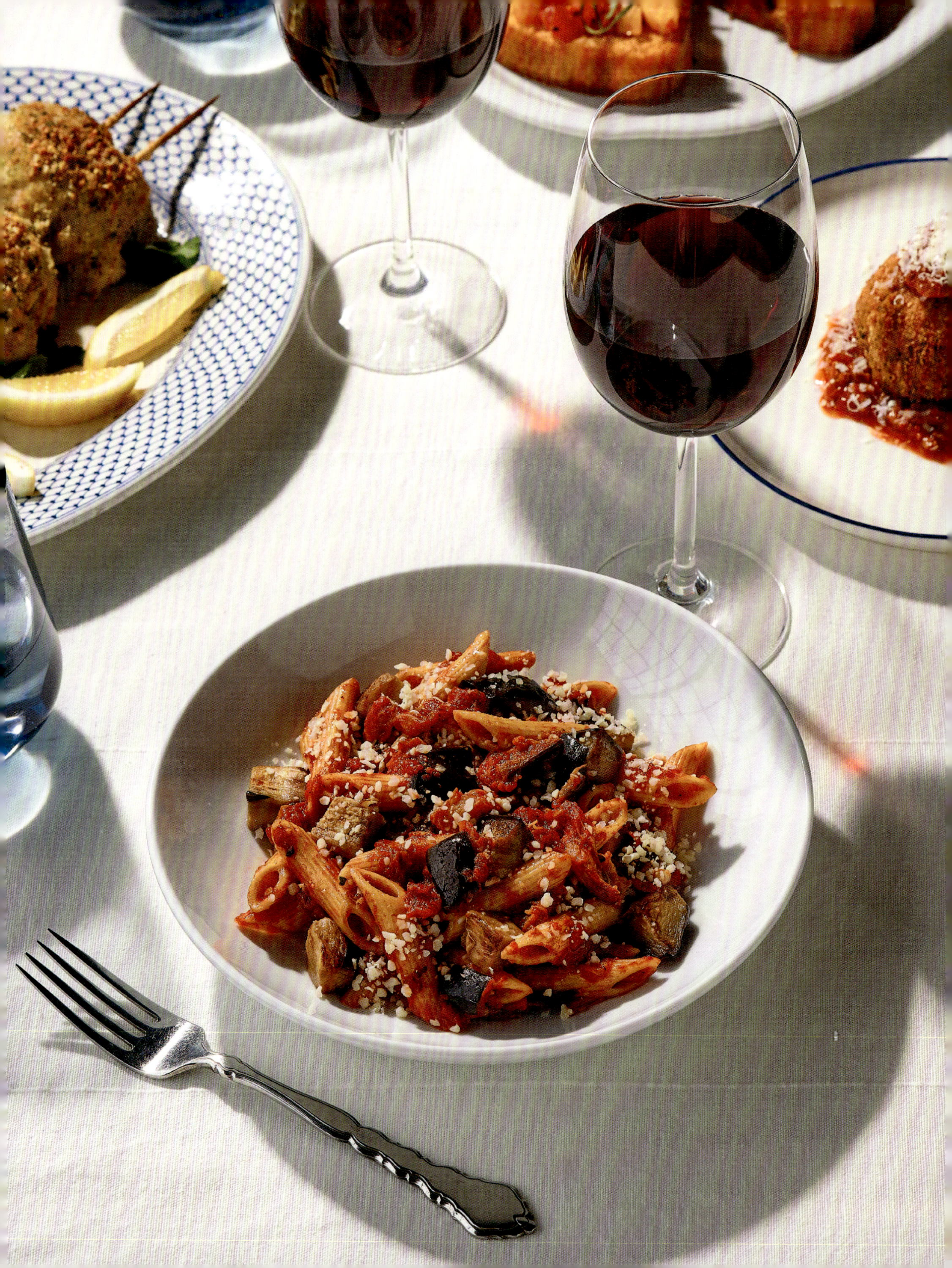

YIELD:
SERVES 4

TIME:
30 MINUTES

- ½ cup white wine
- ¼ cup raisins
- Pinch of saffron threads
- 4 tablespoons olive oil
- 2 tablespoons unsalted butter
- ½ cup breadcrumbs
- ½ teaspoon kosher salt, plus a pinch and more for cooking pasta
- ¼ teaspoon black pepper, plus a pinch
- 1 pound bucatini
- 1 small yellow onion, finely chopped
- 1 small fennel bulb, trimmed and finely chopped, fronds reserved and finely chopped
- 3 cloves garlic, finely chopped
- ½ cup pine nuts, toasted
- 1 pound boneless sardine fillets (fresh or canned), cut into 2-inch pieces

Pasta con le Sarde

Pasta con le Sarde is to Sicily what Carbonara is to Lazio, what Bolognese is to Bologna, and what Pesto alla Genovese is to Liguria. It is an iconic, regional pasta dish that highlights a Sicilian favorite: the humble sardine. The typical preparation of this dish features a wine sauce, sweetened with raisins and loaded with aromatic fennel and a dash of fragrant saffron. We consider it a *must* for travelers looking to learn about local flavors.

In a small saucepan, bring the wine to a simmer over medium-low heat. Remove from the heat and stir in the raisins and saffron. Set aside.

In a small saucepan over medium heat, heat 1 tablespoon of the olive oil and the butter until the butter foams. Add the breadcrumbs and cook, stirring occasionally, until browned, 3 to 5 minutes. Transfer to a small bowl. Season with a pinch of salt and pepper and stir to combine.

Bring a large pot of salted water to a boil over high heat. Add the bucatini and cook according to the package instructions until al dente.

In a large skillet over medium heat, heat the remaining 3 tablespoons of olive oil until shimmering. Add the onion, fennel bulb, ½ teaspoon of kosher salt, and ¼ teaspoon of black pepper. Cook, stirring occasionally, until the onions are tender and translucent, 8 to 12 minutes.

Add the garlic. Stir constantly for 1 minute, then add the pine nuts and sardines and cook just until the sardines are heated through, 2 to 3 minutes. Taste and season with salt and pepper as desired.

Drain the pasta, reserving about 1 cup of the pasta water. Transfer the bucatini to the skillet along with ½ cup of the pasta water. Toss and stir to coat until the sauce is emulsified and thickened and clings to the pasta. If the pasta is too dry, add a splash of water.

Fold in about three-quarters of the reserved fennel fronds. Divide the pasta among four bowls and top with the breadcrumbs and remaining fennel fronds.

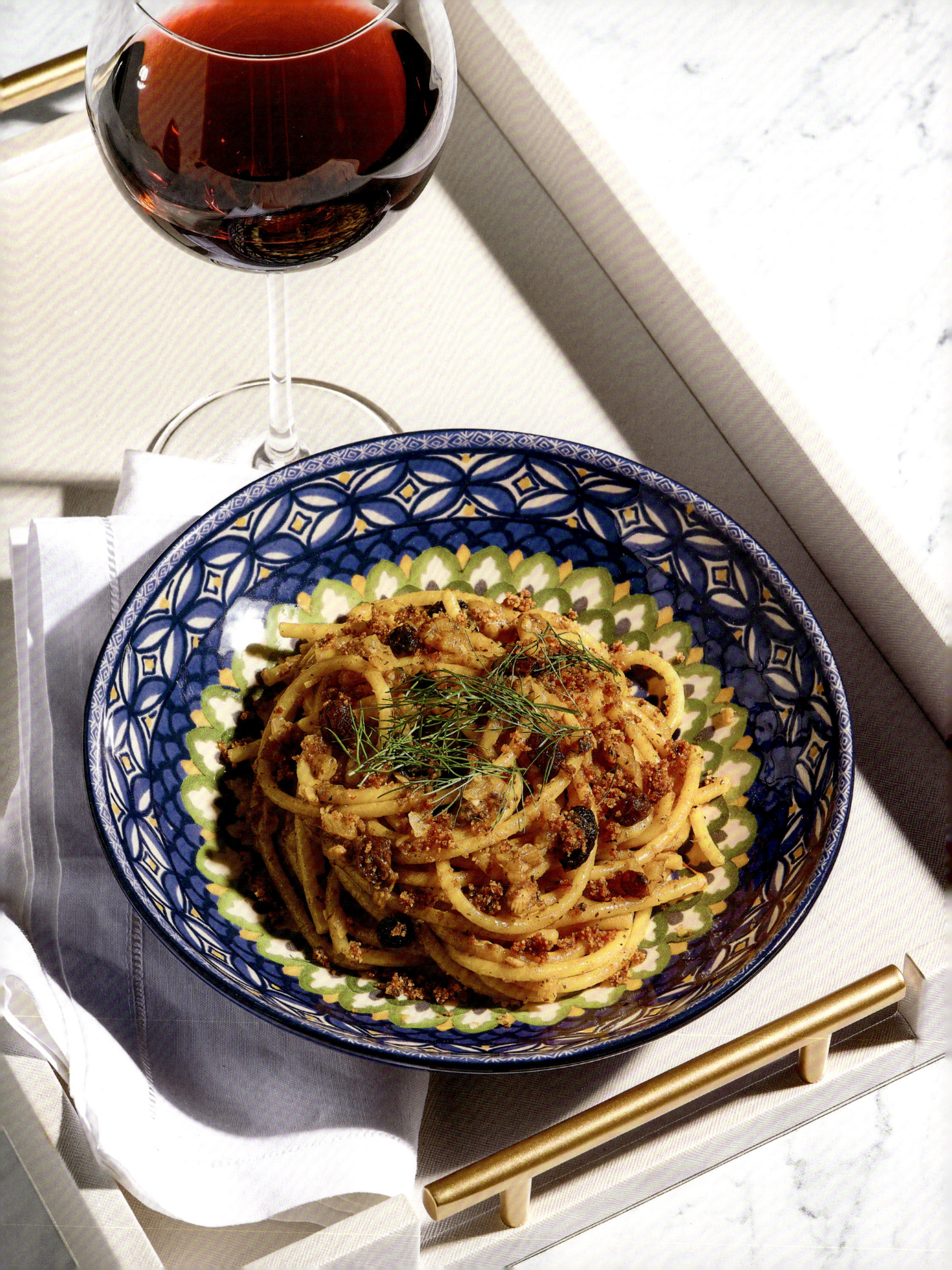

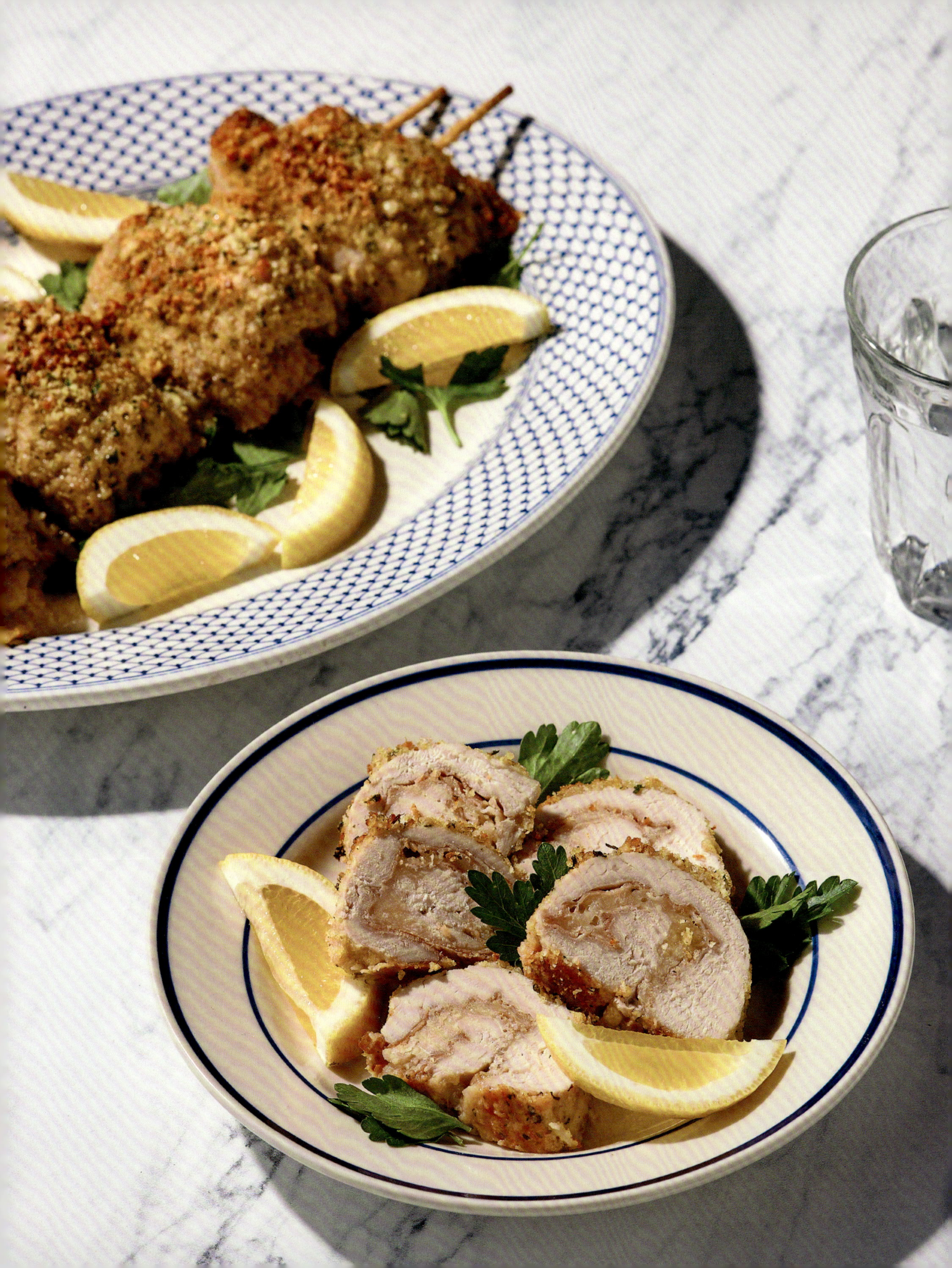

YIELD:
SERVES 4

TIME:
30 MINUTES

8 pork cutlets (about 1 pound), pounded ¼ inch thick

2 tablespoons extra virgin olive oil

Kosher salt

Black pepper

2 cloves garlic, chopped

2 tablespoons chopped parsley

1 teaspoon lemon zest

1 cup breadcrumbs

½ cup grated Parmigiano-Reggiano cheese

½ cup grated Pecorino Romano cheese

4 slices prosciutto

4 ounces aged provolone or smoked mozzarella

Lemon wedges, for serving

Special Equipment

Gas or charcoal grill (optional)

Food processor

Bamboo or metal skewers

Braciole Messinesi

There are so many ways to make braciole, we'd be hard-pressed to determine a wrong way. That said, we understand our guests come to us expecting *discernment*. Know that we take that responsibility seriously in presenting this take on a beloved dish. As the name suggests, our recipe comes from the northeast harbor city of Messina. You'll find the foundational elements represented: a meat cutlet filled with cheese. What really sets Braciole Messinesi apart from other recipes is that it is breaded *and* grilled, which gives it a delicious smoky flavor. Our version includes a cheeky bit of prosciutto, nestled along with the cheese inside the cutlet.

Prepare a gas or charcoal grill, or preheat the oven to 450°F, with the rack in the upper third.

Brush the cutlets with the olive oil on both sides. Season liberally with salt and pepper.

In the bowl of a food processor, combine the garlic, parsley, and lemon zest. Pulse until finely chopped. Add the breadcrumbs and both cheeses and pulse just until combined. Transfer to a wide, shallow bowl.

Press the cutlets into the breading, coating both sides. Transfer the cutlets to a tray. Reserve the remaining breadcrumbs.

Tear the prosciutto slices in half to fit the cutlets and lay a piece on each cutlet. Cut the provolone to fit on the cutlets. Alternatively, shred the cheese and divide among the cutlets evenly.

Roll each cutlet up, tucking the edges over the cheese as you roll, so that the cheese and prosciutto are sealed inside the roll (this is similar to rolling an eggroll or burrito). Thread the rolled cutlets onto skewers (two cutlets per skewer), using the skewers to secure the seams of the rolled cutlets. Pat the reserved breadcrumbs on the tops of the cutlets.

Grill or roast the cutlets until cooked through and the breadcrumbs are golden and crisp, 8 to 10 minutes, flipping halfway through. Serve hot with lemon wedges.

YIELD:
MAKES 24

TIME:
35 MINUTES

GF, V

- 2½ cups almond flour
- 1¼ cups powdered sugar
- ½ teaspoon kosher salt
- 1 teaspoon orange zest (optional)
- 2 large egg whites
- 1 teaspoon pure vanilla extract
- 1 teaspoon almond extract
- 24 raw almonds

Pasta di Mandorla Cookies

If you've taken an opportunity to explore the bakeries and shops that surround our hotel and resort, you've likely already come across these delicious cookies. They are a signature sweet treat. The cute and playful little divot at the center of each one is typically filled with either a whole almond or candied fruit, like a cherry. We like using nuts ourselves, because the name tells you exactly what to expect: *mandorla* or "almond." Even so, there's one thing you may not expect: how quickly these little cookies tend to disappear.

Preheat the oven to 350°F. Line a half-sheet pan with parchment paper.

In a medium bowl, whisk together the almond flour, 1 cup of the powdered sugar, salt, and orange zest (if using). Add the egg whites, vanilla, and almond extract. Stir until a smooth dough forms.

Place the remaining ¼ cup of powdered sugar in a small shallow bowl. Use a 1-tablespoon measuring spoon to scoop the dough and roll it into small balls. Roll the balls in the powdered sugar, shake off the excess, and transfer to the prepared sheet pan.

Press a small divot in the center of each cookie with your thumb. Gently press a single almond into the divot.

Bake for 18 to 22 minutes, or until the cookies are set and golden on the bottom. Cool the cookies in the pan for 10 minutes, then transfer to a wire rack to cool completely. The cookies will keep for up to 1 week in a sealed container at room temperature.

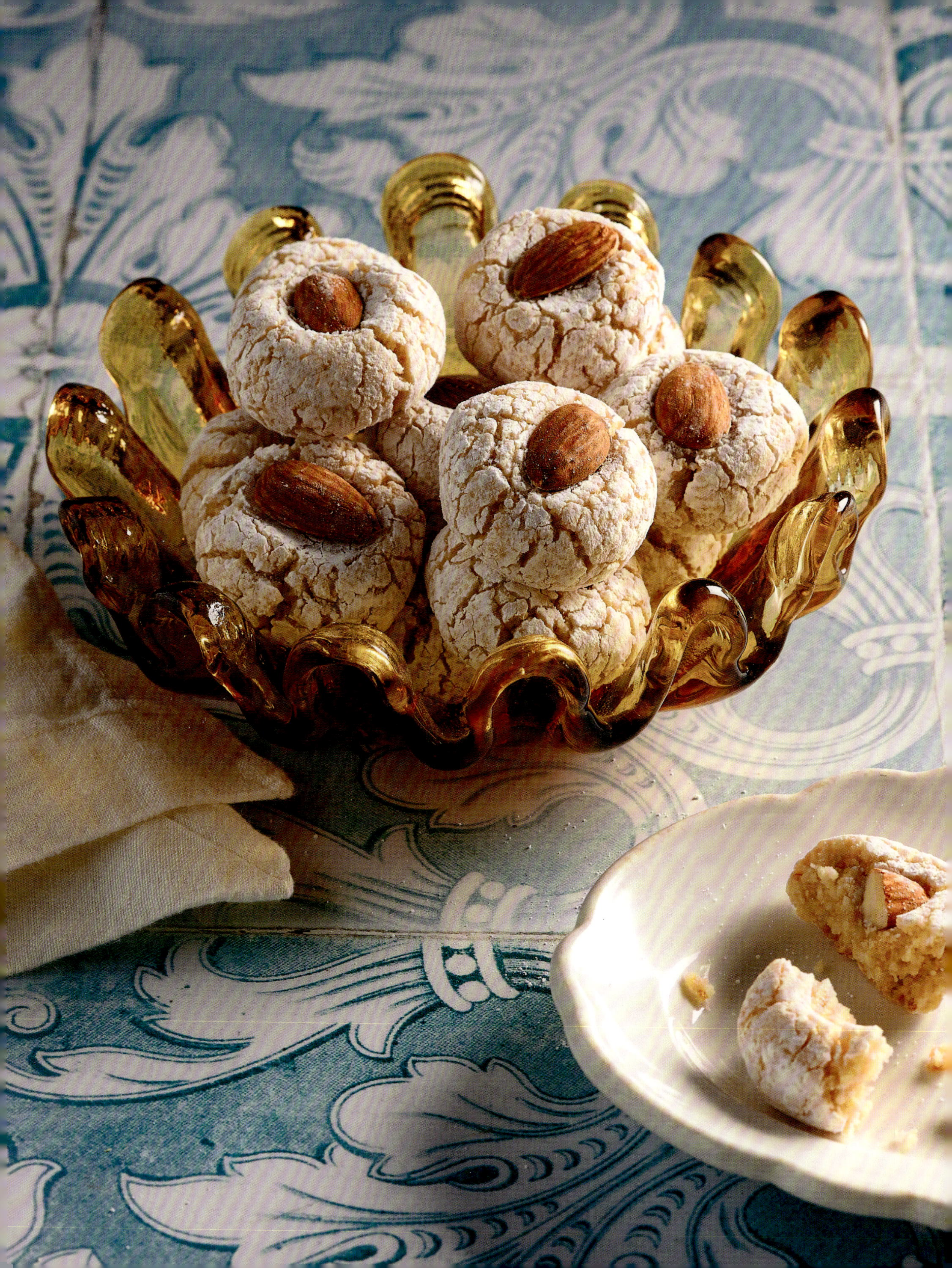

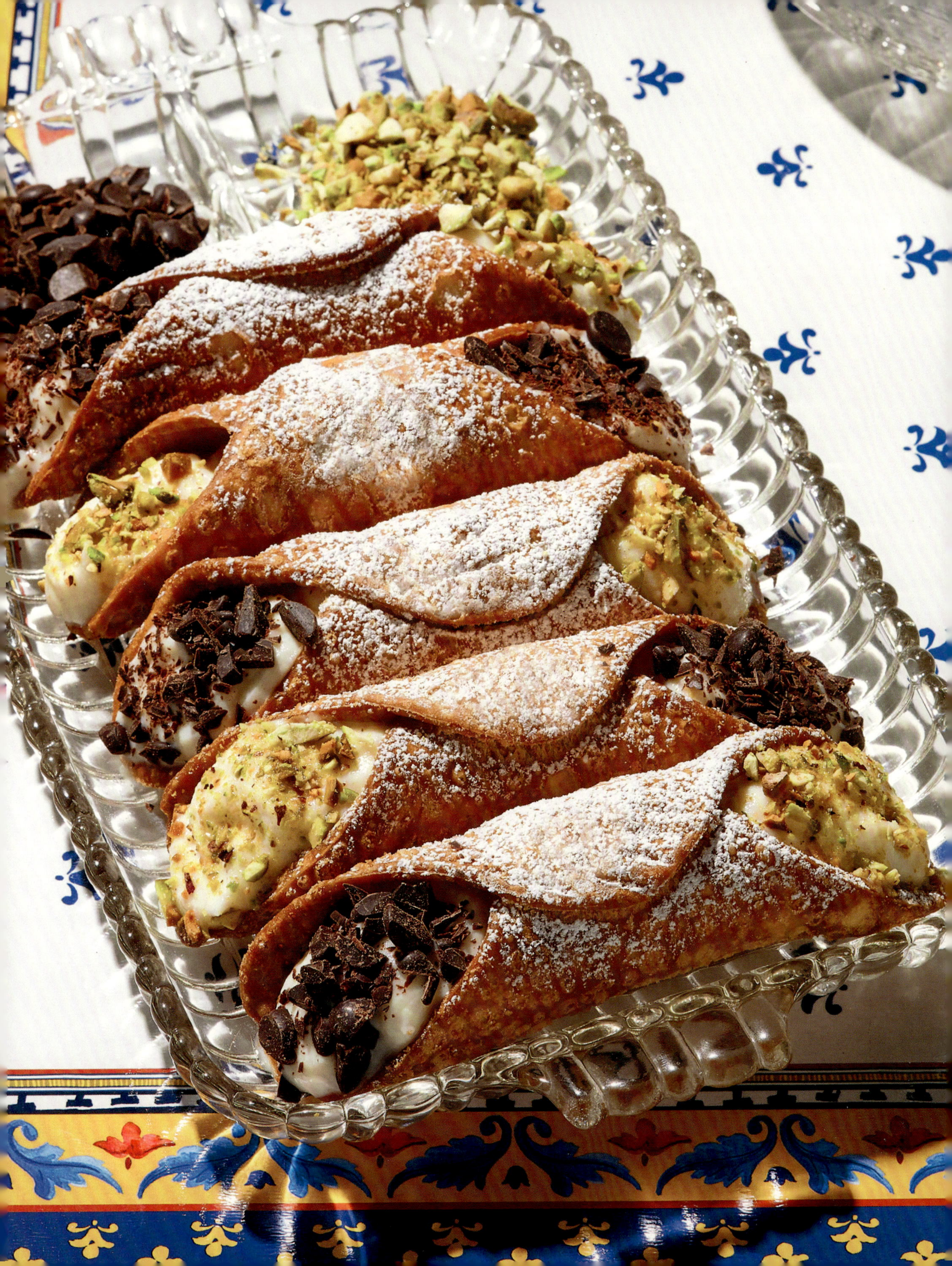

YIELD:
MAKES 24

TIME:
1½ HOURS, PLUS
2 TO 24 HOURS
RESTING

V

Shells
1½ cups 00 flour, plus more for rolling

1½ tablespoons granulated sugar

¾ teaspoon kosher salt

¼ teaspoon ground cinnamon

2 tablespoons vegetable shortening or lard

1 large egg

¼ cup white wine or water

Filling
3 cups full-fat ricotta, preferably sheep's milk (or cow's milk)

¾ cup superfine sugar

1 teaspoon finely grated orange zest

¼ teaspoon salt

For Assembly
8 cups shortening

1 large egg

1 tablespoon water

For Serving
Mini chocolate chips (optional)

Finely chopped pistachios (optional)

Special Equipment
Food processor

Cheesecloth or fine-mesh strainer

Cooking thermometer

Dutch oven

Cannoli tube molds

Piping bag

Cannoli

If you've asked one of our concierges about local desserts, remember that Sicily is the birthplace of this iconic Italian treat. A cinnamon-flavored, shatteringly crisp pastry shell is filled to bursting with sweetened ricotta mixed with myriad optional flavors and fillings. Cannoli from Messina typically feature candied orange, while those from Catania often incorporate pistachios. The shells can be made ahead but shouldn't be filled until the very last moment before serving. Although variations on the fillings are acceptable and encouraged, soggy cannoli are unforgivable.

To make the shells: In the bowl of a food processor, combine the flour, granulated sugar, salt, and cinnamon. Pulse until combined. Add the shortening. Pulse until the texture resembles wet sand. Add the egg and wine. Process on low speed until a soft, wet dough forms.

Grease a large bowl. Scrape the dough into the bowl, cover, and let rest for 2 hours, or refrigerate for up to 24 hours, removing the dough 1 to 2 hours before shaping (the dough should be at room temperature).

To make the filling: If your ricotta is quite soft or runny, layer cheesecloth in a fine-mesh strainer set over a bowl. Add the ricotta, cover, and refrigerate. Let it drain until the ricotta is the consistency of sour cream (it should hold its shape). If you're in a hurry, you can layer the cheesecloth (two or three layers should do it), bundle up the ricotta, then twist and squeeze excess moisture out.

Discard the liquid from the bowl, remove the cheesecloth, and press the ricotta through the strainer using a rubber spatula. Add the superfine sugar, orange zest, and salt. Cover and refrigerate until ready to use.

Transfer the dough to a lightly floured work surface. Roll it out to about ¼ inch thick. Use the top of a drinking glass to cut out as many 2-inch circles as you can. Gather the scraps, reroll, and repeat. (You should wind up with about 24 circles.)

Roll out each circle of dough into a roughly 5½-inch oval. The ovals should be as thin as possible, so that they are almost translucent. Dust with flour to prevent from sticking.

To assemble: In a Dutch oven over medium heat, heat the shortening to 350°F. Line a half-sheet pan with a few layers of paper towels. While the shortening heats, grease the cannoli tube molds.

In a small bowl, beat the egg and water until uniform. Shake off excess flour from an oval of dough and wrap it around a cannoli mold. Brush the seam edges with the egg wash to seal them. Repeat until you've shaped 5 or 6 cannoli (depending on how many tube molds you have).

Use tongs to gently drop the molds into the hot shortening. Fry until golden, bubbly, and crisp, 2 to 3 minutes. Use the tongs to transfer the cannoli to the prepared sheet pan. Let them cool before carefully removing them from the molds.

Repeat the process until you've used up all of the dough. Once cooled, keep the cannoli shells in a sealed container at room temperature for up to 3 days.

When ready to serve, fill a piping bag with the filling. Cut the tip of the bag or use a 1-inch tip (either should be slightly smaller than the cannoli openings). Fill each cannoli at both ends, until completely filled. Dip the ends of each in mini chocolate chips or chopped pistachios, as desired. Serve immediately.

YIELD:
MAKES 1 QUART

TIME:
30 MINUTES, PLUS
6 HOURS CHILLING

GF, V

- 1¼ cups sugar
- 3 tablespoons cornstarch
- ½ teaspoon kosher salt
- 2 cups whole milk
- 1 cup heavy cream
- 7 ounces unsweetened pistachio paste
- 2 teaspoons pure vanilla extract
- ½ teaspoon almond extract

Special Equipment
Fine-mesh strainer
Ice cream maker

Gelato di Pistacchio

Like many matters of the culinary arts, gelato's true origin is up for debate. Some say that a Sicilian chef was the inventor of modern gelato, while others credit chefs from Florence. What we can all agree upon, however, is that there are few things better than a bowl of gelato after a meal. Or any time, if we're being completely honest with ourselves. To make this recipe, it's important to use an unsweetened pistachio paste that is made of pure pistachios and nothing else. If all you can find is sweetened pistachio cream, you'll need to reduce the sugar considerably.

In a medium saucepan, whisk together the sugar, cornstarch, and salt until no clumps remain. Whisk in the milk and heavy cream until smooth.

Place the saucepan over medium heat. Whisk constantly until the mixture thickens and begins to bubble, 8 to 10 minutes. Once it bubbles, set a 1-minute timer and whisk vigorously. Remove from the heat after 1 minute.

In a large, heatproof bowl, combine the pistachio paste, vanilla, and almond extract. Set a fine-mesh strainer over the bowl. Pour the milk mixture through the strainer, pushing it through with a rubber spatula. Discard any solid bits.

Whisk the gelato base until smooth. Cover with plastic wrap, pushing the plastic down to cling to the surface (this prevents a skin from forming). Refrigerate for at least 6 hours.

Churn the gelato base in an ice cream maker according to the manufacturer's instructions. When the gelato is a smooth texture and has just set up, with no ice crystals, transfer to a sealable freezer-safe container.

NOTE

Homemade gelato is best enjoyed as soon as it's made, but it will keep in the freezer for up to 1 month. This recipe stays relatively soft when stored in the freezer. Leave it out for about 10 minutes before serving, for the best texture.

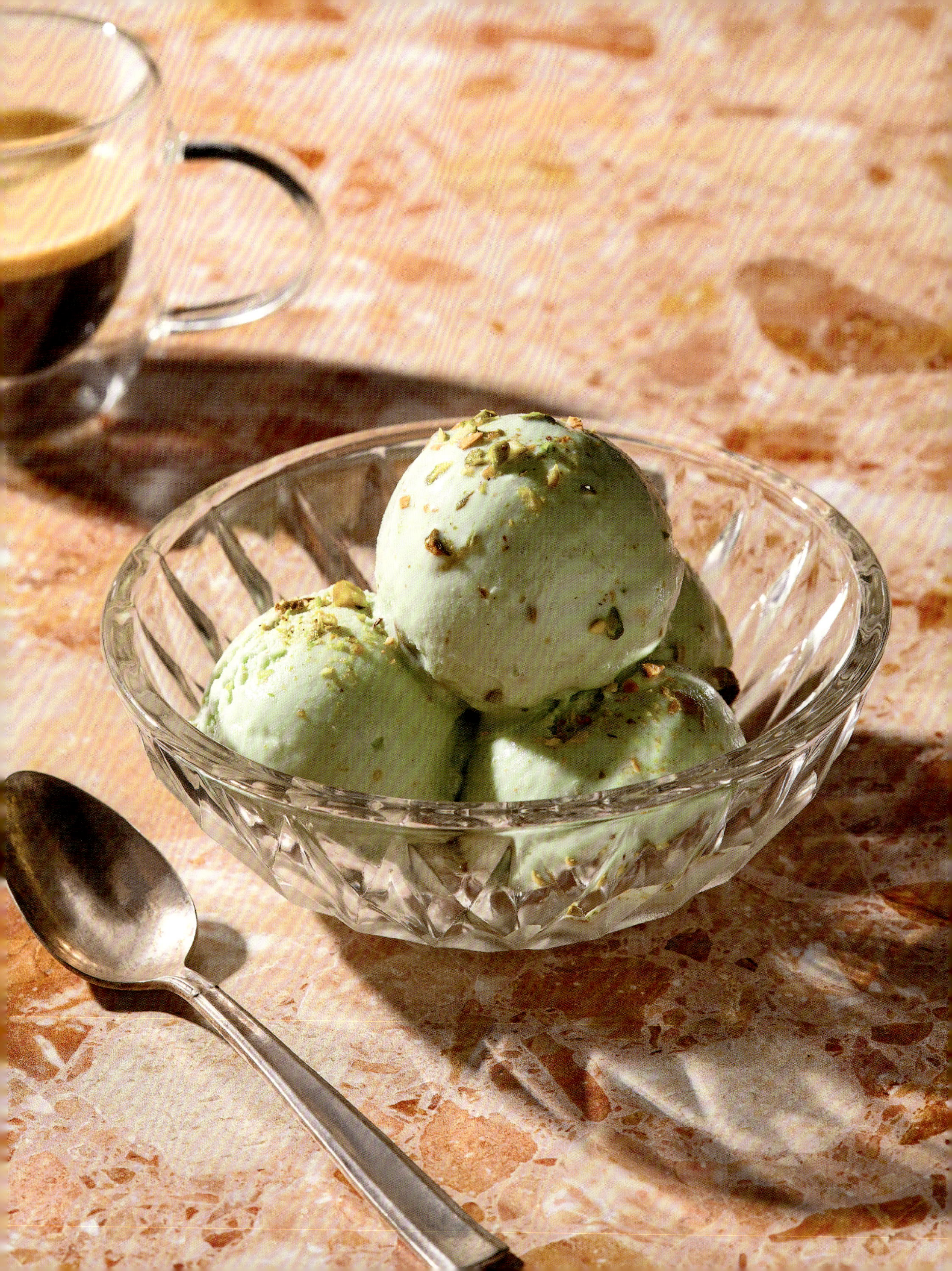

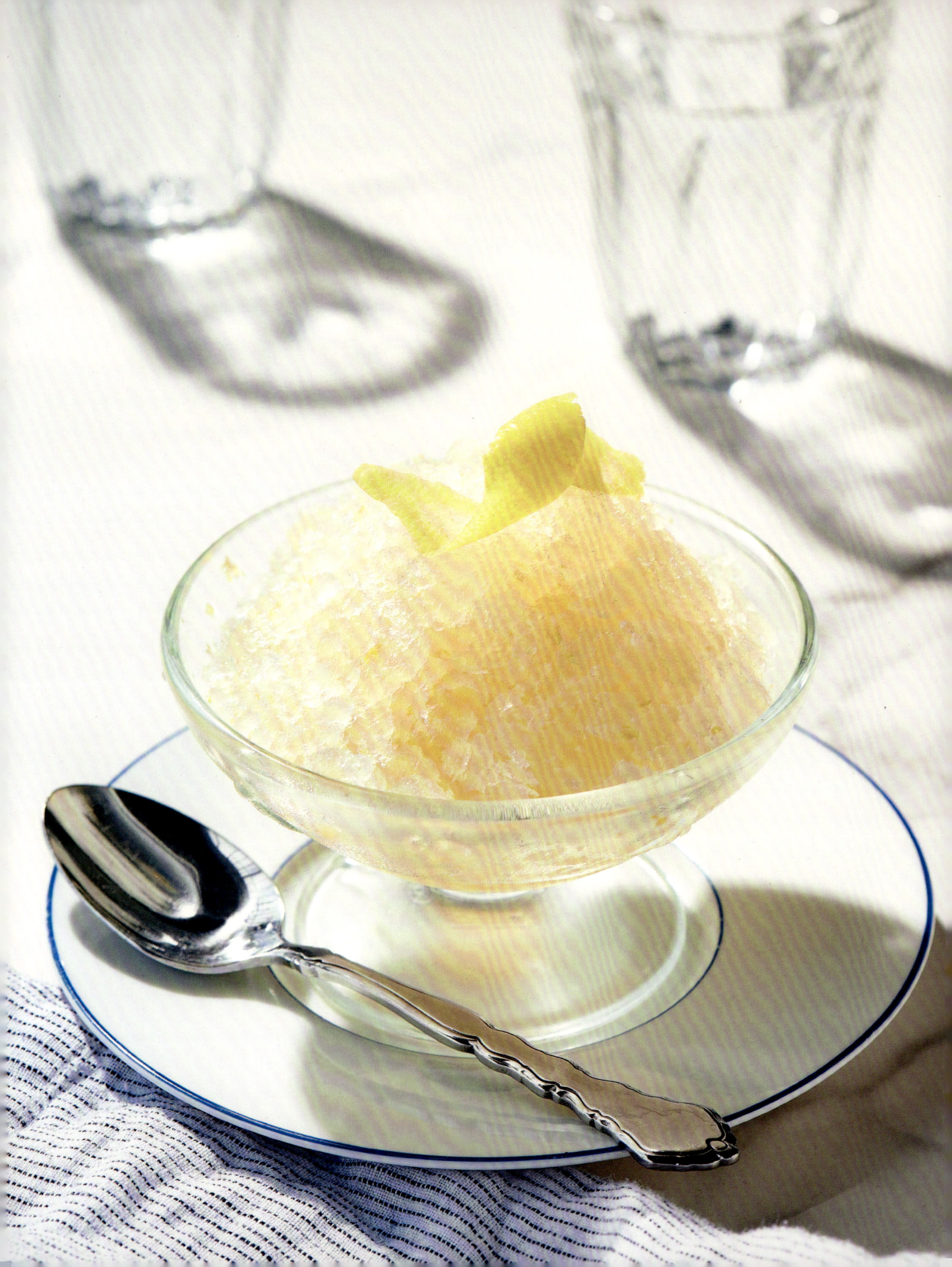

YIELD:
SERVES 4 TO 6

TIME:
6 HOURS

GF, V

- 1 cup warm water
- 3 tablespoons honey
- ⅓ cup sugar
- ¼ teaspoon kosher salt
- 2½ cups prosecco
- ¼ cup fresh lemon juice
- 1 teaspoon finely grated lemon zest

Lemon Prosecco Granita

Clean, bright citrus and bubbly prosecco scream summertime, don't they? And that's what this granita will taste like—a refreshing splash of sunshine in every bite. Like our Coffee Granita (page 55), this treat is an excellent way to enjoy any moment of your vacation. It's a wonderful brunch item, almost like a mimosa or Bellini, but frozen. It is also a lovely way to finish a meal. It's even perfect between courses as a little palate cleanser.

In a large bowl, whisk together the water, honey, sugar, and salt until dissolved. Stir in the prosecco, lemon juice, and lemon zest.

Pour the mixture into a 2-quart, freezer-safe container or a metal baking pan. Cover and freeze for 30 minutes. Stir, breaking up any clumps of ice that have formed at the edges and corners of the container.

Repeat every 30 to 45 minutes, for 6 hours or until the mixture is completely frozen and no longer wet or slushy. It should resemble shaved ice. For the best texture, enjoy the granita within a few days.

YIELD:
SERVES 6 TO 8

TIME:
2 HOURS

V

Dough
4 cups all-purpose flour, plus more for rolling

2 tablespoons granulated sugar

12 egg yolks

¼ cup dark rum

2 tablespoons vegetable shortening

For Frying
8 cups vegetable shortening

Chocolate Glaze
2 cups unsweetened cocoa powder

¼ teaspoon kosher salt

½ cup unsalted butter

2 cups powdered sugar

2 teaspoons pure vanilla extract

2 tablespoons water, plus more as needed

Lemon Glaze
4 cups powdered sugar

2 large egg whites

3 to 4 tablespoons fresh lemon juice

¼ teaspoon kosher salt

Special Equipment
Stand mixer with dough hook attachment

Bench scraper (optional)

Dutch oven

Cooking thermometer

Heatproof mixing bowl

Handheld mixer

Pignolata

Plain pignolata are not unlike struffoli: tiny, golden, fried pastry balls. They can be served with honey and nuts or a variety of other toppings. This Sicilian preparation enrobes the diminutive pastries in dark chocolate and lemon icings, then presses them together. Pignolata are often presented as bricks of pastry, so they can be served to a small group. However, this recipe makes individual servings for everyone invited to your table, because not everybody enjoys sharing. If we wouldn't ask it of our guests, we certainly wouldn't expect you to ask it of yours.

To make the dough: In the bowl of a stand mixer fitted with the dough hook attachment, combine the flour, granulated sugar, egg yolks, rum, and shortening. Mix on low speed until the flour is moistened. Increase the speed to medium and mix until a smooth, uniform dough forms, 6 to 8 minutes.

Transfer the dough to a lightly floured work surface. Divide into two roughly equal portions. Roll one into a rope that is ¼ to ½ inch thick. Use a bench scraper or knife to cut pieces that are about ½ to ¾ inch long. Repeat with the second portion. Gently drape the dough with a clean tea towel to prevent it from drying out.

To fry the dough: In a Dutch oven over medium to medium-high heat, heat the shortening to 375°F. Line a half-sheet pan with aluminum foil, and set a wire rack in the sheet pan.

Fry the dough pieces a couple handfuls at a time (see Note on crowding the oil on page 68). Gently stir the pignolata with a wire skimmer as they fry to prevent them from sticking together. Fry for 2 to 3 minutes, or until golden brown. Transfer to the wire rack. Repeat with the remaining dough.

To make the chocolate glaze: In a medium saucepan over low heat, combine the cocoa powder, salt, and butter. Stir constantly until the butter melts and forms a paste with the cocoa. Remove from the heat and add the powdered sugar, stirring until smooth. Add the vanilla and water and stir until smooth and thickened. If the mixture becomes too thick, add more water, a little at a time, and stir until smooth. It should be thick but pourable and smooth. Set aside.

To make the lemon glaze: In a medium heatproof mixing bowl, combine 3½ cups of the powdered sugar, egg whites, 2 tablespoons of the lemon juice, and the salt.

Bring 1 inch of water to a simmer in a medium saucepan. Set the mixing bowl over the simmering water and stir the mixture with a rubber spatula until smooth and no longer grainy.

Remove the bowl from the heat and use a handheld mixer to beat in the remaining ½ cup of powdered sugar and remaining 1 to 2 tablespoons of lemon juice to taste until the glaze is smooth, thick, and pourable. It should be the same consistency as the chocolate glaze.

To assemble: Line a half-sheet pan with parchment paper. Divide the pignolata between two large bowls. Transfer the chocolate glaze to one bowl and the lemon glaze to the other. Use rubber spatulas to gently toss the pignolata (taking care to not break them apart) in each glaze until well coated.

Make 6 to 8 mounds of the chocolate-covered pignolata on the sheet pan. Divide the lemon-glazed pignolata evenly, mounding each portion right against the chocolate ones.

Gently press the lemon and chocolate mounds together with spoons, rubber spatulas, or gloved hands. Let sit at room temperature for at least 1 hour, or until the glazes set. The pignolata will keep for up to 5 days in a sealed container at room temperature.

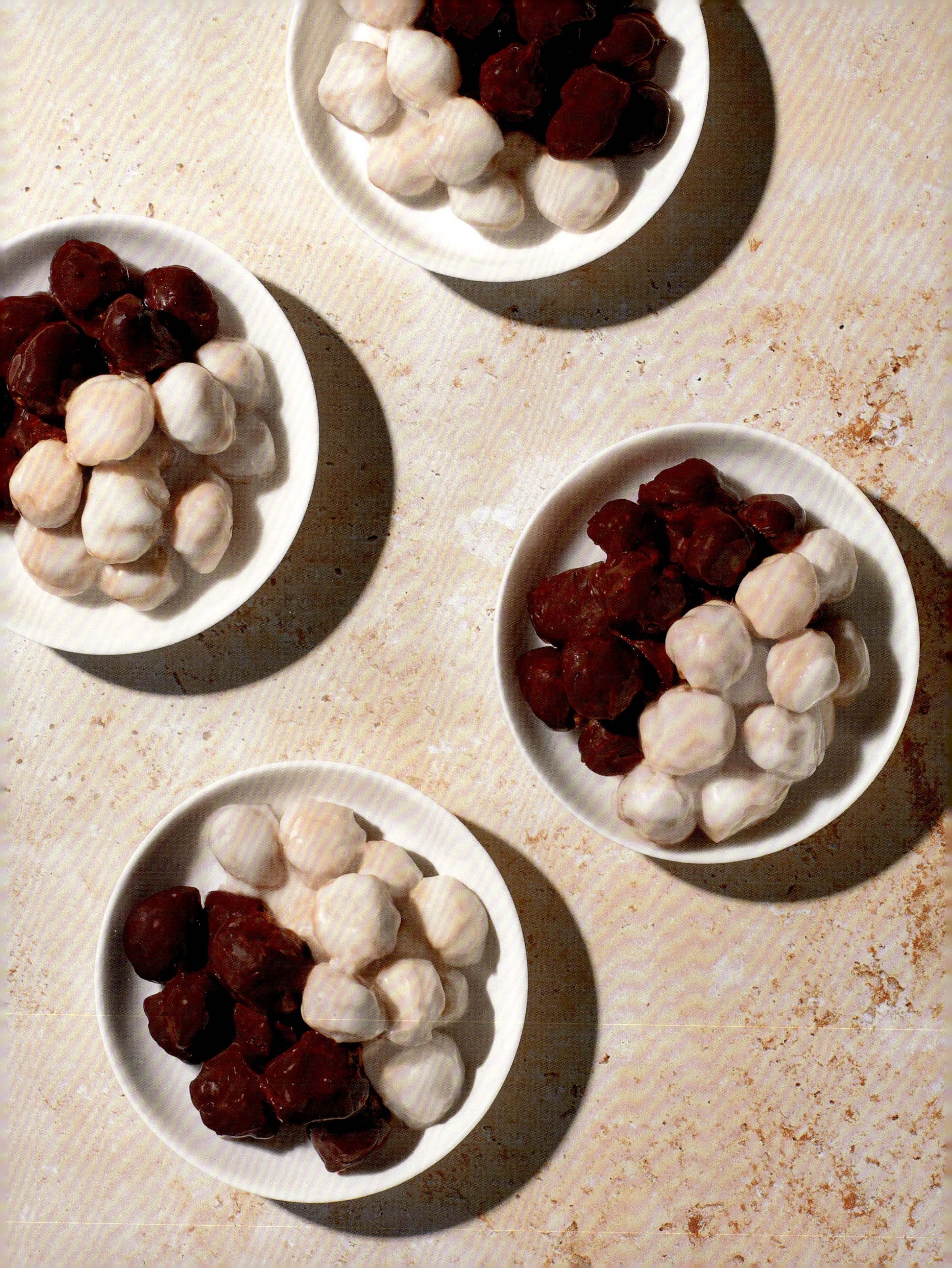

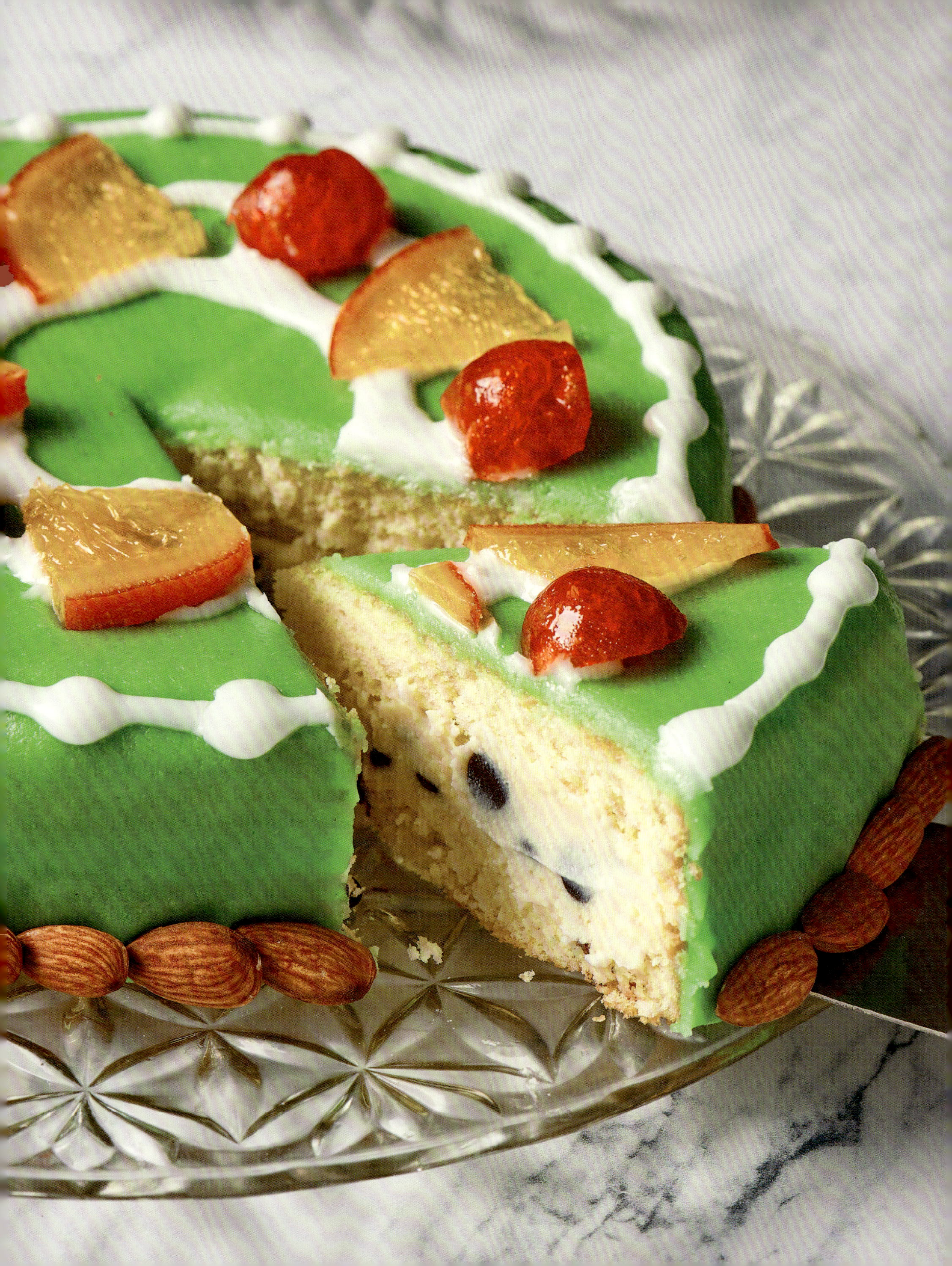

YIELD:
SERVES 8 TO 12

TIME:
1½ HOURS, PLUS 1 HOUR COOLING

V

Cake
6 large eggs
¾ cup superfine sugar
¼ teaspoon kosher salt
1 teaspoon finely grated orange zest
1 tablespoon pure vanilla extract
1¼ cups cake flour, sifted

Simple Syrup
½ cup dark rum
2 tablespoons honey
2 tablespoons granulated sugar

Filling
2 cups ricotta (sheep's milk or whole cow's milk)
1 cup superfine sugar
2 teaspoons pure vanilla extract
¼ teaspoon orange blossom water
½ cup mini chocolate chips

Royal Icing
2 cups powdered sugar, plus more as needed
2 teaspoons meringue powder
1 teaspoon clear vanilla extract
2 tablespoons water
2 tablespoons heavy cream, plus more as needed

Decoration
8 ounces marzipan
2 to 4 drops light green gel food coloring
¼ cup powdered sugar
Candied orange peel
Candied citron peel
Candied cherries
Almonds

Special Equipment
Two 8-inch cake pans
Stand mixer with whisk attachment
Fine-mesh strainer
Handheld mixer
Piping bag

Cassata

At first blush, Cassata cakes may remind you of our Cannoli (page 83). The filling between the layers is quite similar—a sweetened ricotta studded with chocolate. However, the cake layers bring something entirely new to the table. They are delicate and airy and brushed with a simple syrup made with rum (though other spirits can be used). The entire cake is covered in marzipan and decorated with royal icing and candied fruit. Cassata is commonly served at Easter, but we like to make it available as an everyday dessert. After all, we want our guests to feel like every day is a holiday.

To make the cake: Preheat the oven to 350°F. Grease two 8-inch cake pans and line the bottoms with circles of parchment paper.

In the bowl of a stand mixer fitted with a whisk attachment, beat the eggs on medium-low speed until foamy. Add the superfine sugar, salt, orange zest, and vanilla. Increase the speed to medium-high. Beat until the eggs have tripled in volume, 5 to 8 minutes.

Carefully fold in the flour to avoid deflating the batter. Divide the batter evenly between the prepared cake pans. Bake for 18 to 22 minutes, or until golden brown and a toothpick inserted into the center of a cake comes out clean. Let cool in the pan for 10 minutes, then turn out onto a wire rack to cool completely.

To make the simple syrup: While the cakes cool, in a small saucepan over high heat, combine the rum, honey, and granulated sugar. Bring to a boil, stirring constantly, until the sugar and honey are dissolved and any alcohol smell has dissipated, about 5 minutes. Let cool to room temperature.

To make the filling: Place a fine-mesh strainer over a medium bowl. Push the ricotta through the strainer with a rubber spatula. Add the superfine sugar, vanilla, orange blossom water, and chocolate chips and stir to combine. Cover and refrigerate until ready to use.

To make the royal icing: Add the powdered sugar, meringue powder, vanilla, water, and heavy cream to a large bowl. Beat with a handheld mixer on high speed until smooth and thick but still pourable—it should have the consistency of lava, flowing slowly and eventually holding its shape. If it is too thin, add more powdered sugar, and if it's too thick, add more heavy cream. Add this to a piping bag.

To make the decoration: Knead the marzipan together with the food coloring until it's a uniformly pale green. Dust a clean work surface with the powdered sugar and roll the marzipan into a rough circle about ⅛ inch thick.

To assemble the cake: Level the tops of the cakes with a cake leveler or long serrated knife. Brush the cut side of both cakes with the simple syrup. Place one cake layer, cut-side up, on a platter. Top with the filling and smooth into an even layer with an offset spatula. Place the second layer on top, cut-side down.

Drape the marzipan over a rolling pin or your forearm and flop it over the center of the cake. Adjust it and press in place onto the cake. Trim off any excess. Decorate the base of the cake with almonds and the top with the candied fruits. Pipe your preferred decorations on the top with the royal icing. (Decorate more with the royal icing around the sides of the cake, as desired.) Keep the cake covered and refrigerated until ready to serve. The cake will keep for up to 3 days in the refrigerator.

CHAPTER THREE
Thailand

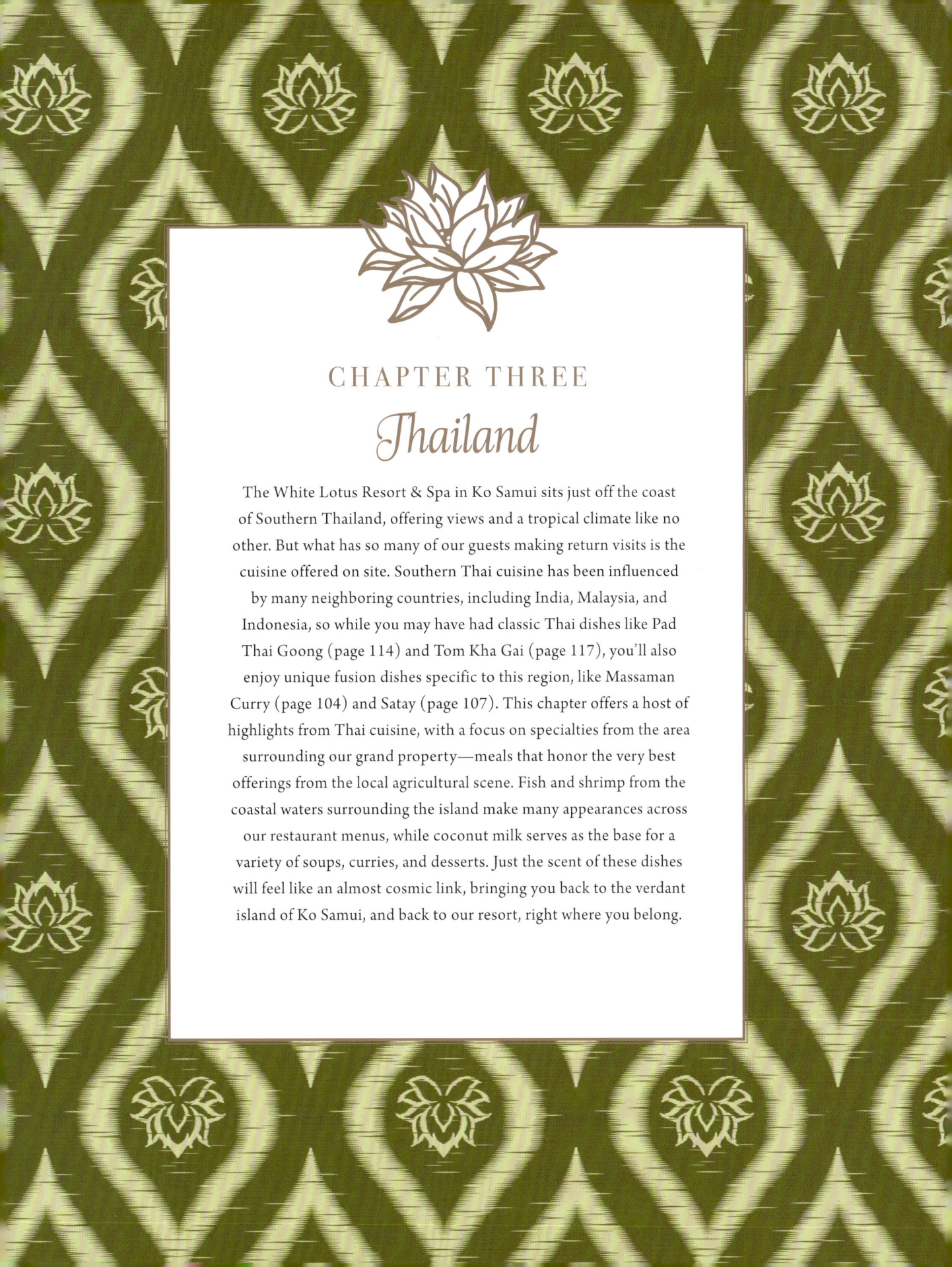

The White Lotus Resort & Spa in Ko Samui sits just off the coast of Southern Thailand, offering views and a tropical climate like no other. But what has so many of our guests making return visits is the cuisine offered on site. Southern Thai cuisine has been influenced by many neighboring countries, including India, Malaysia, and Indonesia, so while you may have had classic Thai dishes like Pad Thai Goong (page 114) and Tom Kha Gai (page 117), you'll also enjoy unique fusion dishes specific to this region, like Massaman Curry (page 104) and Satay (page 107). This chapter offers a host of highlights from Thai cuisine, with a focus on specialties from the area surrounding our grand property—meals that honor the very best offerings from the local agricultural scene. Fish and shrimp from the coastal waters surrounding the island make many appearances across our restaurant menus, while coconut milk serves as the base for a variety of soups, curries, and desserts. Just the scent of these dishes will feel like an almost cosmic link, bringing you back to the verdant island of Ko Samui, and back to our resort, right where you belong.

YIELD:
SERVES 4 TO 6

TIME:
20 MINUTES, PLUS 30 MINUTES MARINATING

Soup
- 4 cloves garlic, peeled
- 4 cilantro roots or 10 stems
- ½ teaspoon white pepper
- 24 medium shrimp, peeled, deveined, and tails removed
- 2 tablespoons vegetable or other neutral oil
- ¼ teaspoon kosher salt
- 6 cups chicken stock
- 4 cups cooked jasmine rice
- 2 tablespoons fish sauce
- 2 tablespoons Thai soy sauce

Toppings
- Soft-boiled eggs
- Chopped cilantro
- Crispy fried scallions
- Fresh ginger, cut into matchsticks
- Lime wedges

Special Equipment
- Food processor
- Dutch oven

MORNING SERVICE

Rice Soup (Khao Tom Goong)

There is something utterly pleasing and comforting about soup at breakfast. And this rice soup fits the role perfectly. A quick morning walk through the streets will reveal a seemingly endless stream of vendors selling this soup in similarly endless variations. Khao Tom Goong can be made with different stocks, including pork, fish, or chicken, as well as different proteins. It can be customized by a wide selection of toppings. Our recipe opts for chicken stock, with the ever-versatile shrimp for protein. However, we know many of our guests prefer to individualize their experiences, which is why we suggest letting each person apply their own toppings.

To make the soup: In the bowl of a food processor, combine the garlic, cilantro roots, and white pepper. Pulse until finely chopped. In a medium bowl, combine half the mixture and the shrimp. Toss until well coated. Cover and refrigerate for 15 to 30 minutes.

In a Dutch oven over medium heat, heat 1 tablespoon of the oil until it shimmers. Add the shrimp and kosher salt, and cook, stirring and tossing occasionally, until the shrimp are cooked through and seared, 3 to 5 minutes. Transfer to a bowl and set aside.

Add the remaining 1 tablespoon of oil to the pot, along with the remaining garlic mixture. Cook, stirring constantly, until fragrant, about 1 minute. Add the chicken stock and bring to a boil over high heat.

Add the rice and cook until warmed through. Stir in the cooked shrimp, fish sauce, and soy sauce. Adjust the seasonings to taste.

To serve: Divide the soup among four to six bowls and serve with the toppings on the side: soft-boiled eggs, chopped cilantro, crispy scallions, ginger matchsticks, and lime wedges; this lets each person garnish to their liking.

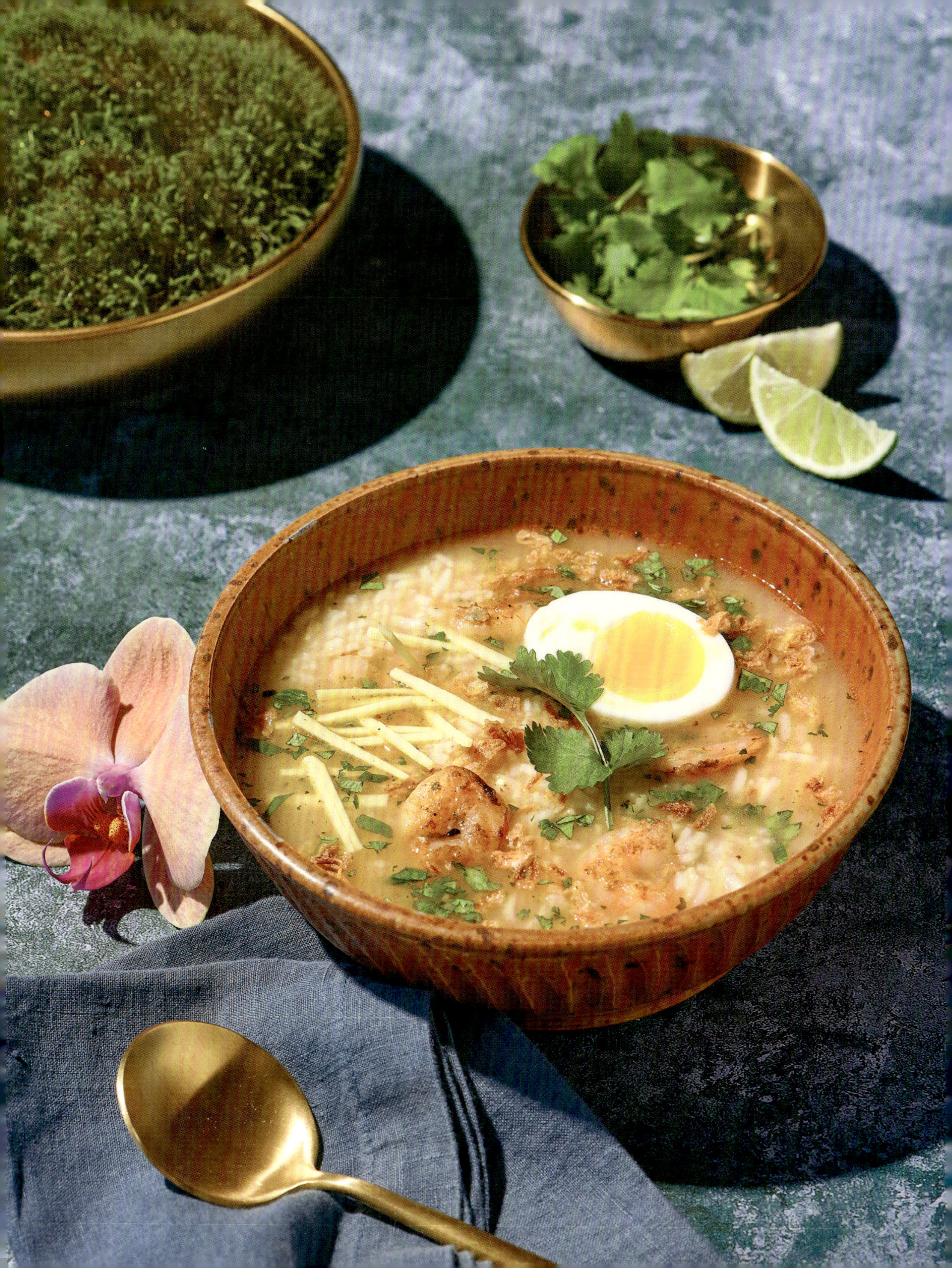

YIELD:
SERVES 4 TO 6

TIME:
75 MINUTES

Soup
2 cloves garlic, peeled
2 cilantro roots or 6 stems
¼ teaspoon white pepper
4 tablespoons Thai soy sauce
1 tablespoon plus 2 teaspoons fish sauce
2 teaspoons palm sugar (see Note)
1 pound ground pork
4 cups chicken stock
3 cups cooked jasmine rice

Toppings
Chopped cilantro
Sliced scallions
Fresh ginger, cut into matchsticks

Special Equipment
Food processor
Dutch oven

Rice Porridge (Jok)

As with Khao Tom Goong (page 94), Jok is a common breakfast soup in Thailand, something you might see street vendors selling in the mornings while you're on a walking tour of the city. It's an evergreen entry on our breakfast menu at the resort. We serve our Jok with delicious pork meatballs for a hearty start to the day. After all, we want to be sure everyone at The White Lotus has what they need to face whatever adventures lie ahead, especially those who don't do naps.

To make the soup: In the bowl of a food processor, combine the garlic, cilantro, white pepper, 2 tablespoons of the soy sauce, 2 teaspoons of the fish sauce, and the palm sugar. Pulse until combined and finely chopped.

Crumble the pork into a large bowl. Add the garlic mixture and use your hands to mix the pork with the seasonings until well combined, sticky, and smooth. Refrigerate until ready to use.

In a Dutch oven, combine the chicken stock, rice, remaining 2 tablespoons of soy sauce, and remaining 1 tablespoon of fish sauce. Bring to a boil over high heat, then decrease to a simmer and cook, stirring occasionally, until the rice breaks down and the porridge becomes quite thick, 30 to 45 minutes. Adjust the seasonings as needed.

Use a 1-tablespoon measure to scoop meatballs into the broth (you should end up with 20 to 24 meatballs). Simmer, stirring, until the meatballs are cooked through, 5 to 10 minutes.

To serve: Divide the soup and meatballs evenly among four to six bowls and serve with the toppings on the side: chopped cilantro, scallions, and ginger matchsticks; this lets each person garnish to their liking.

NOTE

Some palm sugar comes in hard pucks, and some comes in tubs and is quite soft. If you use the former, use a knife to shave off thin slices and chop it finely before measuring.

YIELD:
SERVES 4

TIME:
10 MINUTES

GF, V

- 8 large eggs
- 1½ tablespoons fresh lime juice
- 1½ tablespoons fish sauce
- 1 cup vegetable or other neutral oil
- 2 cups cooked jasmine rice
- Sriracha, for serving (optional)

Special Equipment
Wok

Thai-Style Omelet (Khao Khai Chiao)

Many tourists assume these Thai omelets are solely a breakfast food. Although they may help even the most determined night owls greet the day with a bit more pep, Khao Khai Chiao really is an anytime meal. A signature part of the dish is in the preparation: Eggs seasoned with lime juice and fish sauce (or vinegar for more tartness) are drizzled into hot oil in a steady stream. This results in a loosely shaped, puffy omelet with crisp edges. Each one only takes a mere minute to cook, making Khao Khai Chiao the ultimate fast food for our guests on the go.

In a large bowl, combine the eggs, lime juice, and fish sauce and whisk until frothy.

Heat the oil in a well-seasoned wok over medium-high heat. The oil is hot enough when a couple of drops of the egg mixture sizzle and puff up immediately.

Pour one-quarter of the egg batter into the hot oil from about 6 to 12 inches above the wok. Pour in circles to form a disk. It should sizzle and puff up immediately. Let cook for 30 seconds, flip, and cook for 30 seconds more. Transfer to a paper towel–lined plate. Repeat with the remaining egg batter.

Divide the rice among four bowls and top with each with a cooked omelet. Serve with sriracha, if using.

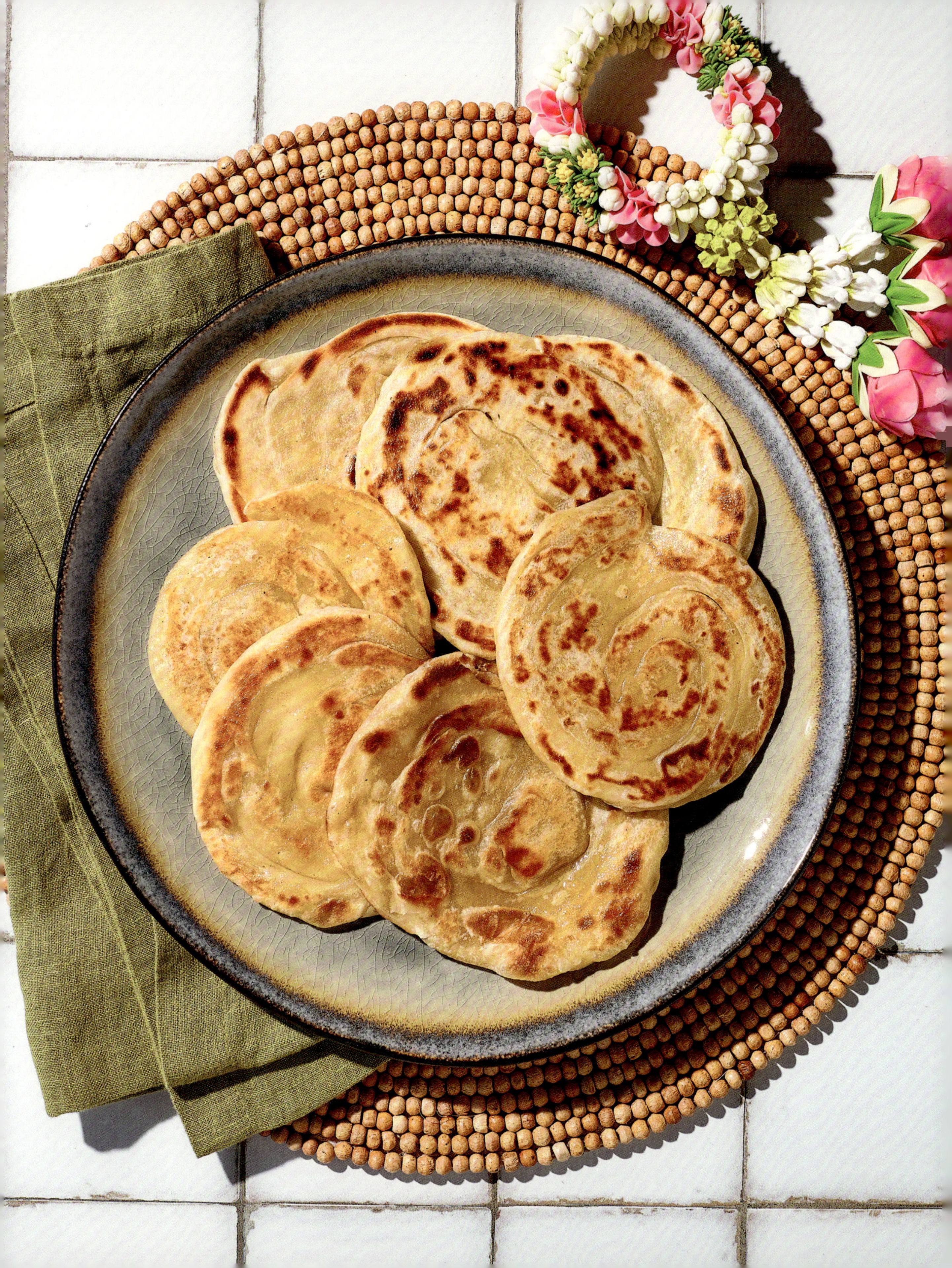

YIELD:
MAKES 6 LARGE ROTI OR 12 SMALL

TIME:
1 HOUR, PLUS UP TO 26 HOURS RESTING

V

- 3 cups all-purpose flour
- 1 tablespoon vegetable or other neutral oil, plus more as needed
- 1½ teaspoons kosher salt
- 1 tablespoon sugar
- 1 large egg
- ¼ cup unsalted butter, softened, plus more for pan
- ¼ cup milk
- ¼ cup warm water

Special Equipment
Stand mixer with dough hook attachment

Roti

Thai roti is the delicious result of combined influences from India and Malaysia. In fact, the discerning palate might recognize in this unleavened flatbread a texture similar to Indian paratha or Malaysian roti canai. It's served throughout Thailand as a snack and can even be incorporated into desserts, like our Roti Pisang (page 126). In Southern Thailand, plain roti may be served with curries, though we know many guests enjoy eating these crispy, flaky flatbreads all on their own.

In the bowl of a stand mixer fitted with the dough hook attachment, combine all the ingredients. Mix on low speed, just until the flour is moistened. Increase the speed to medium and mix until smooth and elastic, about 10 minutes.

Oil a large bowl. Transfer the dough to the bowl and roll it around until completely coated in oil. Cover and refrigerate for 4 hours, and up to 24 hours.

When you're ready to make the roti, let the dough come to room temperature for 2 hours. Divide it into 6 to 12 equal portions.

Place one piece of dough on a well-oiled work surface. Coat it with more oil and use the palm of your hand to flatten the dough as thin as possible. (You should be able to see the work surface through much of the dough.) By the time you're done, the dough should be almost paper-thin. Don't worry if it tears in places.

Coat the bottom of a nonstick skillet with vegetable oil. Heat over medium heat until the oil shimmers.

While the pan heats, pinch the edge of the dough and lift it so that it hangs like a drape over the work surface. Slowly lower it down into a sort of coil, with some folds overlapping on themselves, then tuck the edge you were holding into the bottom. Gently flatten the ruffly coil with your palm to a thickness of about ¼ inch.

Transfer the dough to the heated skillet. Press it gently with a flat, solid spatula. Cook until deep golden brown and puffed, 3 to 4 minutes. Flip and cook for 3 minutes more. Add about 1 teaspoon of butter to the pan. Swirl and coat the roti, then flip and coat the opposite side. Transfer to a wire rack to cool.

Repeat steps 4 through 7 with the remaining dough. While the new roti cooks, hold your hands on either side of the cooked roti on the wire rack. Hold them as if you were about to clap, and then clap. This incorporates air in between the layers and gives the roti a flakier texture. Don't worry if the top crackles a little; that's part of the look. Serve plain or with curry dishes. Roti is best eaten the day it's made.

YIELD:
SERVES 4

TIME:
25 MINUTES

GF

Sour Curry (Kaeng Som)

This elegant preparation of Southern Thai–style curry is known as "sour curry." Yes, it's a sour (but also spicy!) curry with green papaya and chunks of a firm-fleshed fish. It's a delightful dish that seems to prove that less is more. On the other hand, we know more is *also* more. Accordingly, many modern iterations of this dish incorporate a variety of vegetables and shrimp instead of, or in addition to, fish. Naturally, we've gone the extra mile and packed our sour curry with loads of vegetables, shrimp, *and* fish.

To make the curry: In the bowl of a food processor, combine the chiles, salt, shallots, garlic, and shrimp paste. Blend until smooth. If the curry paste needs a little liquid to help it blend, add ¼ to ½ cup of the seafood stock.

Combine the curry paste and remaining stock in a Dutch oven. Bring to a boil over high heat. Add the papaya, daikon, and carrot. Return to a boil, then decrease to a simmer. Simmer, stirring occasionally, until the vegetables are slightly tender but the papaya retains some crunch, 8 to 12 minutes.

Add the long beans, fish, shrimp, fish sauce, 2 tablespoons of the tamarind paste, and 2 tablespoons of the palm sugar. Simmer until just cooked through, 2 to 4 minutes. Add the lime juice. Taste and adjust the seasonings with more tamarind paste, palm sugar, or salt as needed.

To serve: Divide the stew evenly among four bowls. Serve hot with lime wedges and, if desired, cooked jasmine rice on the side. Leftover soup will keep, refrigerated in a sealed container, for up to 3 days.

Curry
- 10 to 15 dried mild and hot chiles (use a mix, adjusted to your heat preference)
- 1 teaspoon kosher salt
- 2 large shallots, peeled
- 6 cloves garlic, peeled
- 2 teaspoons fermented shrimp paste
- 4 cups seafood or fish stock
- 2 green papaya, peeled and thinly sliced
- ½ cup peeled and thinly sliced daikon radish
- 1 medium carrot, peeled and thinly sliced
- 1 cup long beans, cut into 1-inch pieces
- 1 pound barramundi, red snapper, or cod fillets, cut into 2-inch chunks
- 16 large shrimp, peeled and deveined
- 2 tablespoons fish sauce
- 2 to 4 tablespoons tamarind paste
- 2 to 3 tablespoons palm sugar (see Note, page 96)
- 2 tablespoons fresh lime juice

For Serving
- Lime wedges
- Cooked jasmine rice (optional)

Special Equipment
- Food processor
- Dutch oven

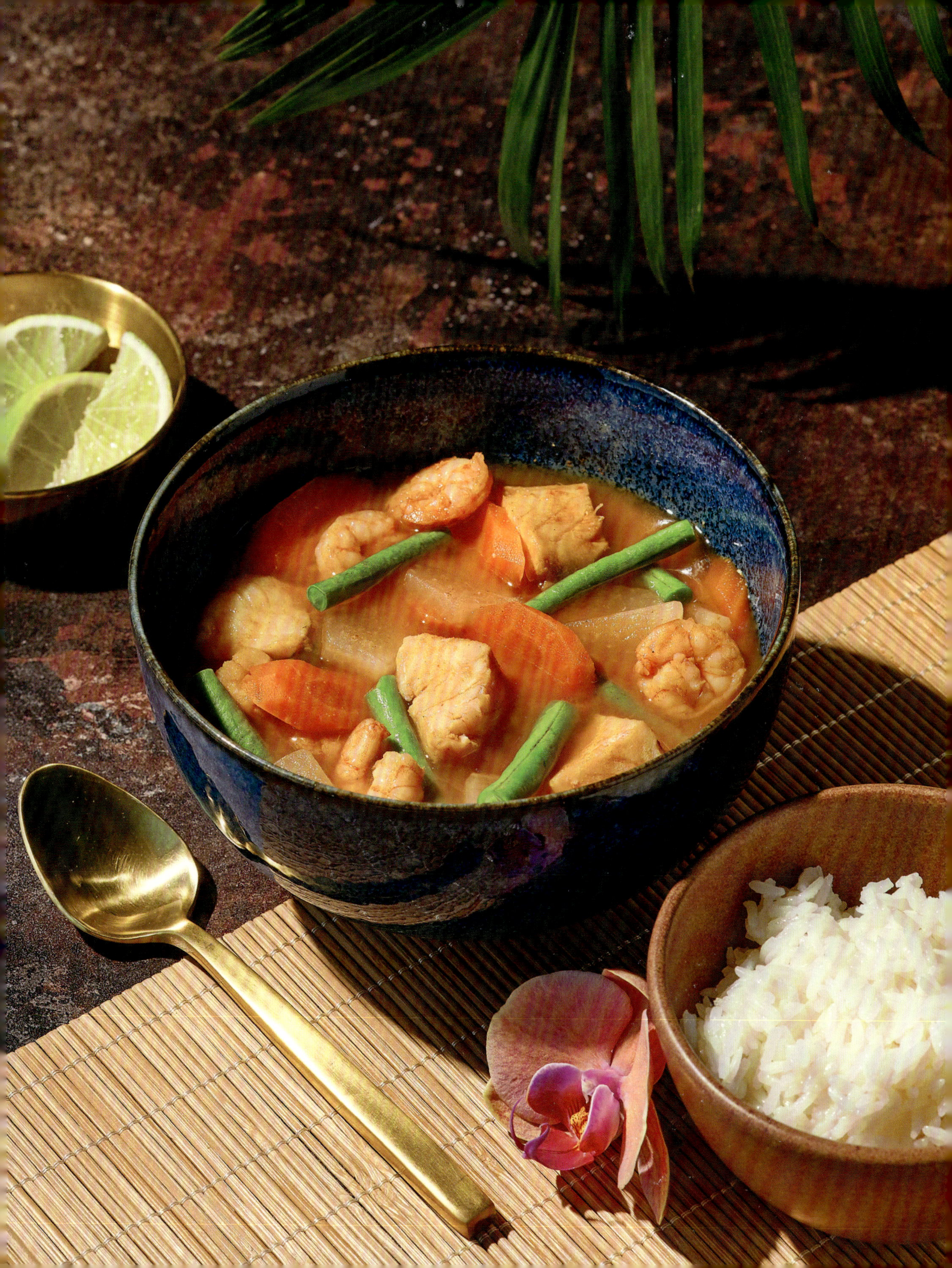

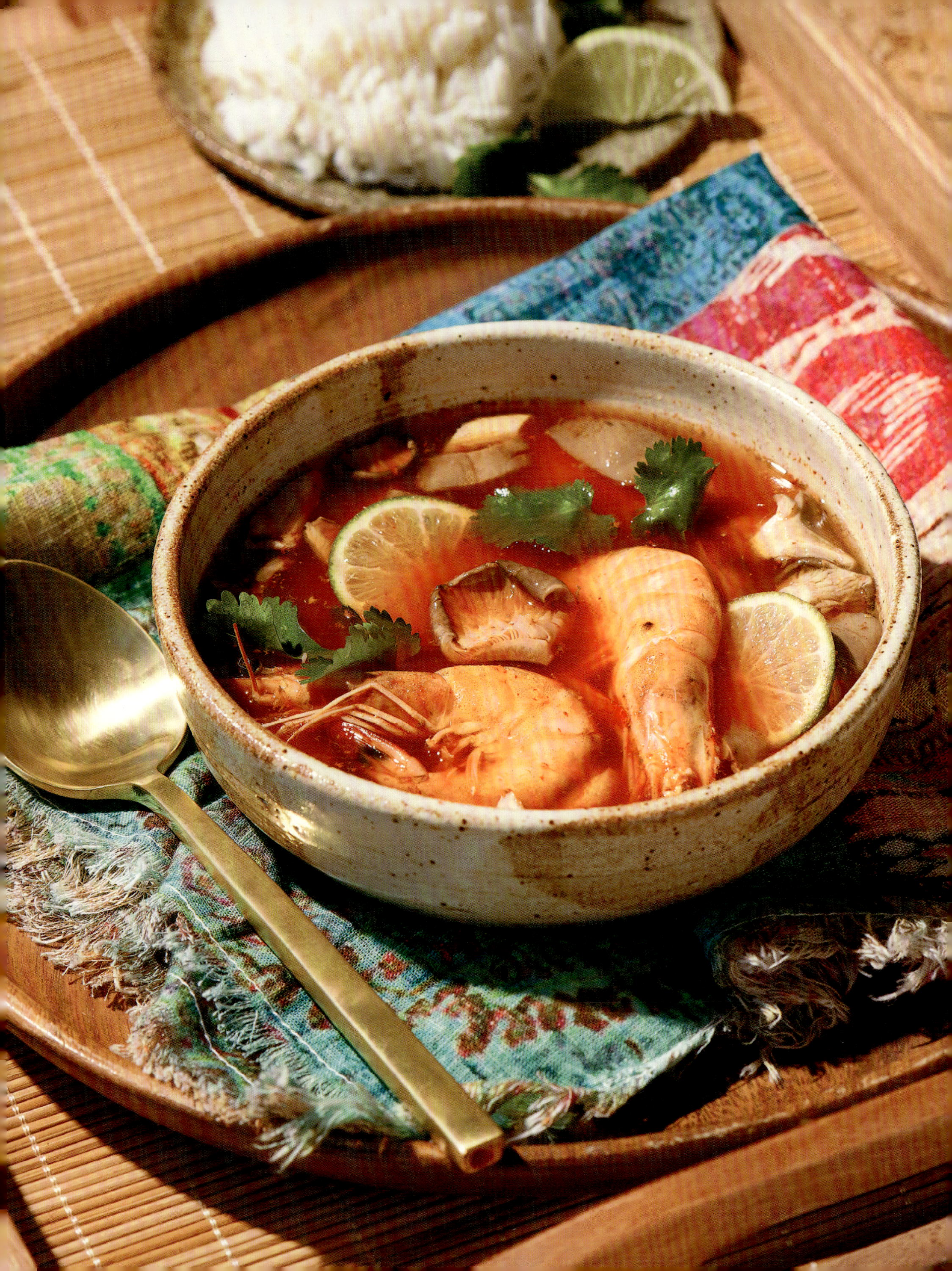

YIELD:
SERVES 4

TIME:
30 MINUTES

Soup
4 cups chicken or fish stock

8 makrut lime leaves, torn and lightly crushed (fresh or frozen, but dry will also work)

2 stalks lemongrass, smashed and cut into 2-inch pieces

One 1-inch piece galangal, thinly sliced

4 Thai bird's eye chiles, sliced and lightly crushed

8 ounces oyster mushrooms, coarsely chopped

2 to 4 tablespoons nam prik pao (Thai chile paste)

¼ cup fish sauce, plus more as needed

2 teaspoons palm sugar (see Note, page 96)

2 pounds prawns, heads and shells on

½ cup fresh lime juice

For Serving
Chopped cilantro

Cooked jasmine rice (optional)

Special Equipment
Dutch oven

Fine-mesh strainer

Tom Yum Goong

To make a proper Tom Yum Goong soup, you must start by infusing your stock with classic Thai aromatics: lime leaves, galangal, and lemongrass. Although it is tradition to leave these in the soup, they are not meant to be eaten. Since not all of our guests bring the same, we'll call it *context*, when they travel, we thought it best to strain those aromatics out before proceeding with the recipe. If you prefer to stick to tradition, as well you should, it may be worth it to advise your guests to avoid eating those aromatics. Serve Tom Yum Goong as a starter without rice, or with, for a heartier meal.

To make the soup: In a Dutch oven, combine the stock, lime leaves, lemongrass, and galangal. Bring to a boil over high heat, then decrease to a simmer. Simmer for 10 minutes. Use a small fine-mesh strainer to remove the lime leaves, lemongrass, and galangal. (You can also strain the infused stock into a bowl and return the strained stock to the pot; whichever is easiest.)

Add the chiles, mushrooms, nam prik pao, fish sauce, and palm sugar. Return to a boil over high heat, then decrease to a simmer. Cook until the mushrooms are tender, 5 to 7 minutes.

Carefully add the prawns and cook, stirring occasionally, until they're cooked through, 2 to 4 minutes. Remove from the heat and stir in the lime juice. Taste and add fish sauce, if needed.

To serve: Divide the soup among four bowls, garnish with the cilantro, and serve with bowls of cooked jasmine rice, if desired.

**YIELD:
SERVES 6 TO 8
TIME:
3 HOURS
GF**

Massaman Curry (Kaeng Massaman)

- 2 tablespoons mild red chile powder
- 2 teaspoons ground coriander
- 1½ teaspoons ground cumin
- 1 teaspoon kosher salt
- 1 teaspoon ground cinnamon
- ½ teaspoon white pepper
- ¼ teaspoon ground cloves
- ¼ teaspoon ground nutmeg
- ¼ teaspoon ground cardamom
- 1 large shallot, coarsely chopped
- 1 stalk lemongrass (bottom half only), coarsely chopped
- 1-inch piece galangal, sliced
- 3 cilantro roots or 8 stems
- 4 cloves garlic, peeled
- 1½ teaspoons fermented shrimp paste
- 2 tablespoons vegetable or other neutral oil
- 2 pounds boneless beef chuck, cut into 2-inch chunks
- 6 cups water
- Two 13.5-ounce cans coconut milk
- 1 small yellow onion, thinly sliced
- ¼ cup roasted, unsalted peanuts
- 1 pound waxy potatoes, cut into 2-inch pieces
- 2 tablespoons palm sugar (see Note, page 96)
- 2 tablespoons fish sauce
- 1 tablespoon tamarind paste
- Cooked jasmine rice, for serving

Special Equipment
Food processor
Dutch oven

As those who have participated in some of our educational offerings may know, this curry is a product of Muslim influence on this region of Thailand. That's one reason it is more commonly made with beef or chicken rather than pork. We adhere to that tradition ourselves, keeping a warm and inviting beef recipe on offer. Massaman curry is on the milder side, making it an excellent choice for those who love all the beautifully aromatic flavors of curry but prefer less heat.

In the bowl of a food processor, combine the chile powder, coriander, cumin, salt, cinnamon, white pepper, cloves, nutmeg, cardamom, shallot, lemongrass, galangal, cilantro roots, garlic, and shrimp paste. Blend until smooth. (As an alternative, you can use 4 ounces of store-bought massaman curry paste.) Set aside.

In a Dutch oven over medium-high heat, heat the oil until shimmering. Working in batches, sear the beef for 3 to 5 minutes on each side until seared all over.

Once all the beef has been seared, return it to the Dutch oven. Add the water and 2 tablespoons of the curry paste. Bring to a boil over high heat, then decrease to a simmer. Cook until the beef is tender, about 2 hours. Transfer to a bowl. (You can do this up to 3 days in advance; refrigerate the beef and cooking liquid in a sealed container. Skim off the fat, and reserve 3 cups of the cooking liquid.)

Wipe out the Dutch oven. Add 1 can of coconut milk. Cook over high heat, stirring occasionally, until thickened and reduced by half, 5 to 8 minutes. Add the remaining curry paste and onion. Cook, stirring constantly, until the fat has separated from the coconut milk and the mixture is sizzling, 5 to 8 minutes.

Add the remaining 1 can of coconut milk and stir until smooth. Return the beef to the pot and add the peanuts, potatoes, palm sugar, fish sauce, and tamarind paste. Add just enough of the beef cooking liquid to keep the ingredients submerged. Bring to a boil, then decrease to a simmer. Cook for 15 to 20 minutes, or until the potatoes are fork-tender.

Serve with bowls of cooked jasmine rice. Leftover curry will keep for 5 days, refrigerated in a sealed container.

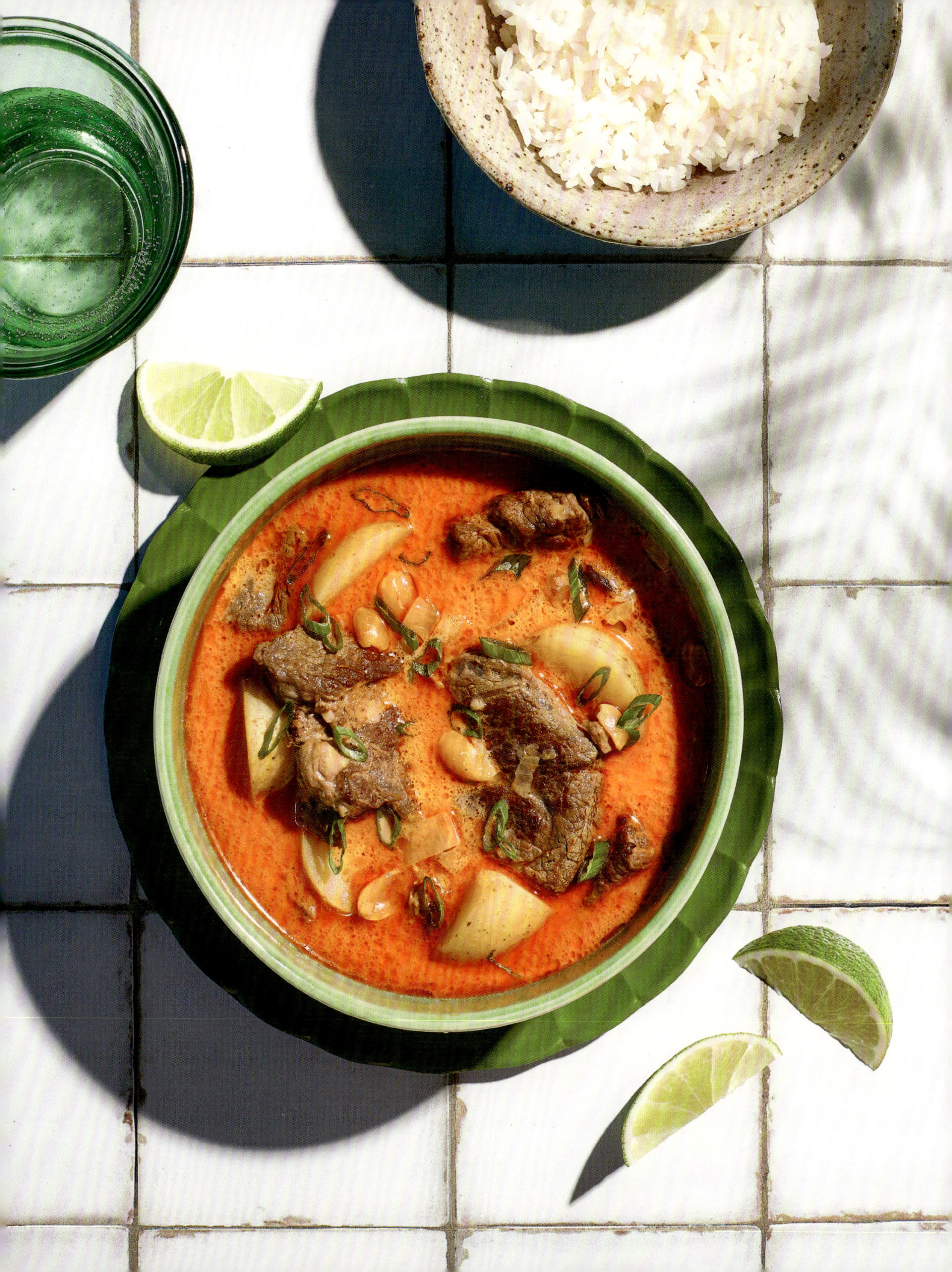

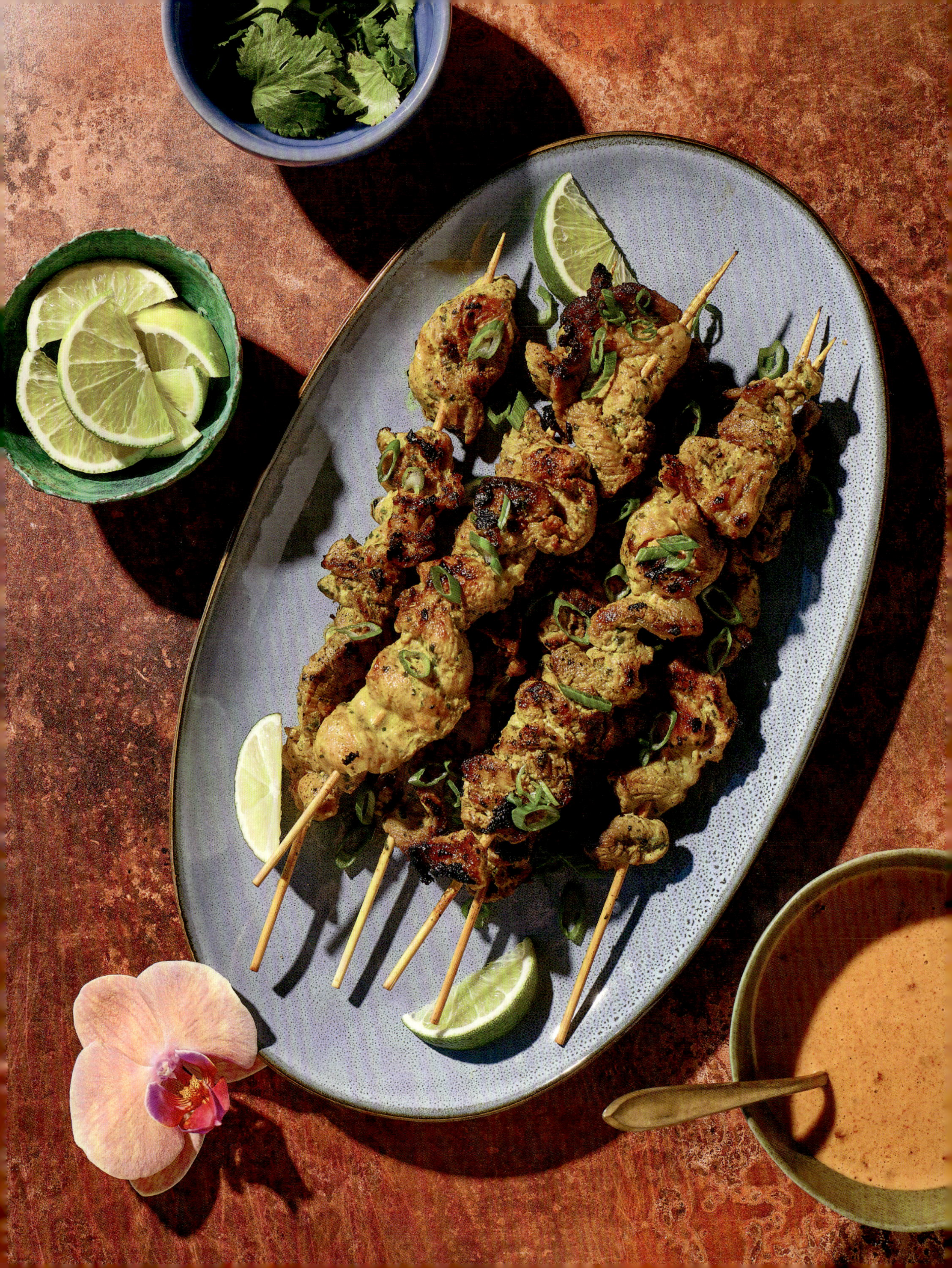

YIELD:
SERVES 4

TIME:
20 MINUTES, PLUS
1 HOUR MARINATING

Pork
1 pound boneless pork shoulder, excess fat trimmed

½ cup coconut milk

¼ cup vegetable or other neutral oil

¼ cup cilantro leaves

2 tablespoons white vinegar

2 teaspoons ground coriander

2 teaspoons ground turmeric

2 teaspoons ground cumin

1 stalk lemongrass (bottom half only), sliced

3 scallions (white and light green parts only), coarsely chopped

2 tablespoons soy sauce

2 tablespoons fish sauce

1 tablespoon fresh grated galangal

1 tablespoon palm sugar (see Note, page 96)

Peanut Sauce
¾ cup roasted, unsalted peanuts

1 cup coconut milk

2 tablespoons red curry paste

2 tablespoons tamarind paste

3 tablespoons palm sugar (see Note, page 96)

1 tablespoon fish sauce

1 tablespoon soy sauce

Juice of 1 lime

Special Equipment
Blender

Food processor or mortar and pestle

Bamboo skewers, soaked in water for 1 hour

Gas or charcoal grill (optional)

Satay

Satay has its roots in Indonesia (Java, specifically), one of many neighboring countries that has had an influence on Thai cuisine. Although it is widely considered the national dish of Indonesia, it remains extremely popular in Thailand, where it is commonly made with pork instead of beef or chicken. Our globe-traveling guests are encouraged to visit our Indonesian location if they'd like to compare the two dishes.

To make the pork: Freeze the pork for about 15 minutes, or until somewhat firm. Slice it into ¼-inch strips about 4 inches long by 1½ inches wide. Transfer to a sealable container.

In a blender, combine the coconut milk, oil, cilantro, vinegar, coriander, turmeric, cumin, lemongrass, scallions, soy sauce, fish sauce, galangal, and palm sugar. Blend until smooth, 3 to 5 minutes. Pour over the pork and seal the container. Let sit for at least 1 hour, and up to 8 hours. If marinating for more than 1 hour, refrigerate until ready to cook.

To make the peanut sauce: Use a food processor or mortar and pestle to grind the peanuts into a fine meal (with some larger chunks still visible). If using a food processor, be careful not to overblend the peanuts into peanut butter.

Scoop the fat from the top of the coconut milk into a small saucepan. Heat over medium-high heat until melted. Add the red curry paste and cook until fragrant and bubbling, 2 to 4 minutes.

Add the rest of the coconut milk and decrease the heat to medium. Add the ground peanuts, tamarind paste, palm sugar, fish sauce, and soy sauce. Taste and adjust the seasonings to your preference. Remove from the heat and squeeze the lime juice over the pan.

Prepare a charcoal or gas grill (or preheat the broiler). While the grill heats, thread 2 or 3 strips of pork onto each bamboo skewer, crowding the pork slightly.

Grill the skewers for 2 minutes, until lightly charred. Flip and grill for 1 minute, or until cooked through. If using a broiler, you may need to adjust the timing here, depending on the strength of your broiler. Serve with the peanut sauce.

THAILAND — MORNING SERVICE

YIELD:
SERVES 4 TO 6

TIME:
1 HOUR

GF

- 6 cloves garlic, peeled
- 2 large shallots, quartered
- 2 tablespoons vegetable or other neutral oil
- 15 jumbo shrimp, deveined, shells and tails on
- 10 Thai chiles, stemmed and coarsely chopped
- 2 tablespoons fresh lime juice
- 1 tablespoon fish sauce
- 1 tablespoon palm sugar (see Note, page 96)
- 4 to 6 cups lightly steamed or raw vegetables, such as broccoli, cauliflower, and sliced cucumbers (optional)

Special Equipment
- Gas or charcoal grill (optional)
- Charcoal (optional)
- Apple, cherry, maple, or hickory wood (optional)
- Smoking tray (optional)
- Grill basket (optional)
- Bamboo or metal skewers (optional)
- Mortar and pestle or food processor

Nam Prik Goong Siap

Shrimp is the star of this salty, tangy, spicy dish. Some variations use dried shrimp, but we rather enjoy this hot, smoked approach. Most of the shrimp works hard behind the scenes, as it's processed with the other ingredients. However, some is set aside to act as a decorative topping. Productive *and* visually striking, this recipe encapsulates our commitment to our guests. Enjoy alongside a variety of steamed and raw vegetables, and remember that our staff is on hand for anything you may need whenever and wherever you choose to stay with us.

Prepare a gas or (preferably) charcoal grill for two-zone heating (half the burners on or the charcoal pushed to one side of the grill). You can also use a broiler.

In a small bowl, combine the garlic, shallots, and 1 tablespoon of the oil. Toss to coat. Make an aluminum foil packet and transfer the garlic and shallots to it, leaving the top slightly open.

Place a chunk of apple, cherry, maple, or hickory wood on the charcoal. (If you're using a gas grill, you'll need a smoking tray and wood chips; if broiling, you will not be able to use wood chips—proceed without them.) Place the foil packet on the cool side of the grill (out of direct heat). Cover the grill and smoke the shallots and garlic for 10 minutes.

Meanwhile, in a large bowl, toss the shrimp with the remaining 1 tablespoon of oil. Transfer the shrimp to a grill basket or skewer them if you don't have a basket. Place the basket or skewers on the cool side of the grill and cover. Smoke for 5 to 7 minutes, or until fully cooked through, flipping once halfway through cooking.

Transfer the foil packet and shrimp to a cutting board and let cool. Transfer the garlic and shallots to a large mortar and pestle or the bowl of a food processor (whichever you use must be large enough to hold the shrimp). Add the Thai chiles and crush or blend until relatively smooth.

Once the shrimp are cool enough to handle, peel them and remove the tails. Place 11 of the shrimp in the mortar and pestle or food processor. Crush or process until smooth (it's okay if the mixture is a little chunky, sort of like store-bought salsa). Add the lime juice, fish sauce, and palm sugar and pulse just until combined.

Transfer the mixture to a serving bowl. Top with the remaining 4 shrimp in a spiral pattern. Serve alongside lightly steamed and raw vegetables, if using.

**YIELD:
SERVES 4

TIME:
45 MINUTES

GF**

- 10 dried spur chiles, stemmed and seeded
- 1 tablespoon coriander seeds
- 2 teaspoons cumin seeds
- 1 teaspoon white peppercorns
- 1½ teaspoons kosher salt
- 1 tablespoon curry powder
- 2 stalks lemongrass (bottom halves only), thinly sliced
- 4-inch piece galangal, sliced
- 2-inch piece ginger, sliced
- 3-inch piece turmeric, sliced
- 8 cloves garlic, peeled
- 1 large shallot, quartered
- Two 13.5-ounce cans coconut milk
- 1 small yellow onion, thinly sliced
- 1 pound yellow potatoes (such as Yukon gold), cut into 2-inch pieces
- 2 tablespoons fish sauce
- 1 tablespoon palm sugar (see Note, page 96)
- 1 tablespoon tamarind paste
- 1 pound boneless, skinless chicken thighs, cut into 1-inch pieces
- Cooked jasmine rice, for serving

Special Equipment
Food processor
Dutch oven
Spice grinder or mortar and pestle

EVENING SERVICE

Yellow Curry (Kaeng Kari)

This bright yellow curry dish originated in Southern Thailand and is considered milder than other Thai curries. It's a beautiful, cozy recipe to make at home because the main ingredients are familiar in many regions of the world: potatoes, chicken, and onions. Although making your own curry paste typically yields the best results, store-bought curry pastes do offer a strong and reliable option. And who doesn't love a shortcut? Of course, the ultimate shortcut would be coming back to the resort and letting our chefs take care of all the cooking.

In a small skillet over medium heat, toast the chiles, coriander, cumin, and peppercorns. Stir constantly until fragrant, 2 to 4 minutes. Remove from the heat, let cool, then grind in a spice grinder or mortar and pestle until finely ground.

In the bowl of a food processor, combine the toasted spices, salt, curry powder, lemongrass, galangal, ginger, turmeric, garlic, and shallot. Pulse until smooth.

Remove the separated cream from one of the cans of coconut milk and heat in a large Dutch oven over medium-high heat until melted. Stir in the curry powder and onion and cook, stirring frequently, until the mixture is sizzling, 5 to 8 minutes. Stir in the remaining coconut milk.

Add the potatoes, fish sauce, palm sugar, and tamarind paste and bring to a boil. Decrease to a simmer and cook, stirring occasionally, until the potatoes are fork-tender, about 15 minutes.

Stir in the chicken and simmer until the chicken is cooked through, 5 to 8 minutes. Taste and add fish sauce or salt as needed. Serve hot with cooked jasmine rice.

YIELD:
SERVES 4 TO 6

TIME:
1½ HOURS, PLUS 8 TO 24 HOURS MARINATING

GF

Chicken Biryani (Khao Mok Gai)

The key to a flavorful Thai approach to a Chicken Biryani is in the marinade. While most marinades are meant to be discarded after they've done their job, this one does double duty. First, it flavors and tenderizes the chicken. Next, it's used to flavor the rice before even adding the stock. We imagine our entrepreneurially minded guests might appreciate the efficiency. This marinade is a reminder that there's beauty in a strong foundation. While this recipe takes some time to get right, it's well worth the investment. Much like working your way up from a Petal to a Blossom Circle member, the benefits are exquisite.

Marinade
- 2 teaspoons ground coriander
- 1 teaspoon ground cumin
- 1 teaspoon ground turmeric
- 1 teaspoon ground cinnamon
- ½ teaspoon white pepper
- ¼ teaspoon black pepper
- ¼ teaspoon ground cardamom
- ¼ teaspoon ground cloves
- 2 cilantro roots or 6 stems
- 6 cloves garlic, peeled
- 2 large shallots, coarsely chopped
- One 3-inch piece fresh ginger, sliced
- 2 teaspoons kosher salt
- 1 tablespoon sugar
- 1 cup plain yogurt

Chicken
- 4 skin-on, bone-in chicken thighs
- 4 skin-on, bone-in chicken drumsticks
- 2 tablespoons vegetable or other neutral oil

Rice
- 2 cups Thai jasmine rice
- 2 bay leaves
- 2 cups chicken stock

Dipping Sauce
- 1 bunch mint, leaves only
- 1 bunch cilantro, leaves and tender stems only
- 2 to 4 Thai green chiles
- ¼ cup white vinegar
- 3 tablespoons sugar
- 1 tablespoon grated ginger
- 2 cloves garlic, peeled
- 1 teaspoon kosher salt

To Serve
- Sliced cucumbers
- Sliced tomatoes
- ½ cup crispy shallots

Special Equipment
- Blender or food processor
- Dutch oven

To make the marinade: In a blender or food processor, combine all the ingredients and blend until smooth.

To make the chicken: Transfer the chicken to a resealable container (a plastic freezer bag works great). Pour the yogurt marinade over the chicken and massage into the chicken to coat. Seal the container and refrigerate for 8 to 24 hours.

To make the rice: Transfer the rice to a large bowl and cover with water. Swish the rice around with your hand for about a minute. Drain the water. Repeat four times, or until the water runs relatively clear. Drain the rice completely.

Remove the chicken from the marinade and wipe off any excess back into the container (do not discard the marinade). Pat the chicken dry with paper towels and place on a clean plate. In a Dutch oven, heat the oil over medium heat until it shimmers. Add the chicken, skin-side down, and leave undisturbed for 3 to 5 minutes, or until well seared. Flip and sear for 3 minutes more. Transfer to a plate. Scrape up any browned bits with a wooden spoon and set aside. Sear the remaining chicken in the same way.

Drain all but 2 tablespoons of the fat from the Dutch oven. Add the rice and reserved marinade. Cook, scraping up any browned bits while stirring. Return the reserved browned bits to the pot and cook until the mixture is fairly dry, 5 to 7 minutes.

Spread the rice into an even layer on the bottom of the Dutch oven. Nestle the chicken, skin-side up, in the rice. Add the bay leaves and chicken stock. Bring to a boil, then decrease to a light simmer over low heat. Cover and cook for 18 to 20 minutes, or until the rice has absorbed the liquid.

To make the dipping sauce: Add all of the ingredients to the bowl of a food processor or blender and blend until smooth. Season to taste with additional salt, sugar, or vinegar, as desired.

To serve: Transfer the chicken to a platter and fluff the rice with a fork. Serve the chicken and rice with the dipping sauce, cucumbers, tomatoes, and crispy shallots.

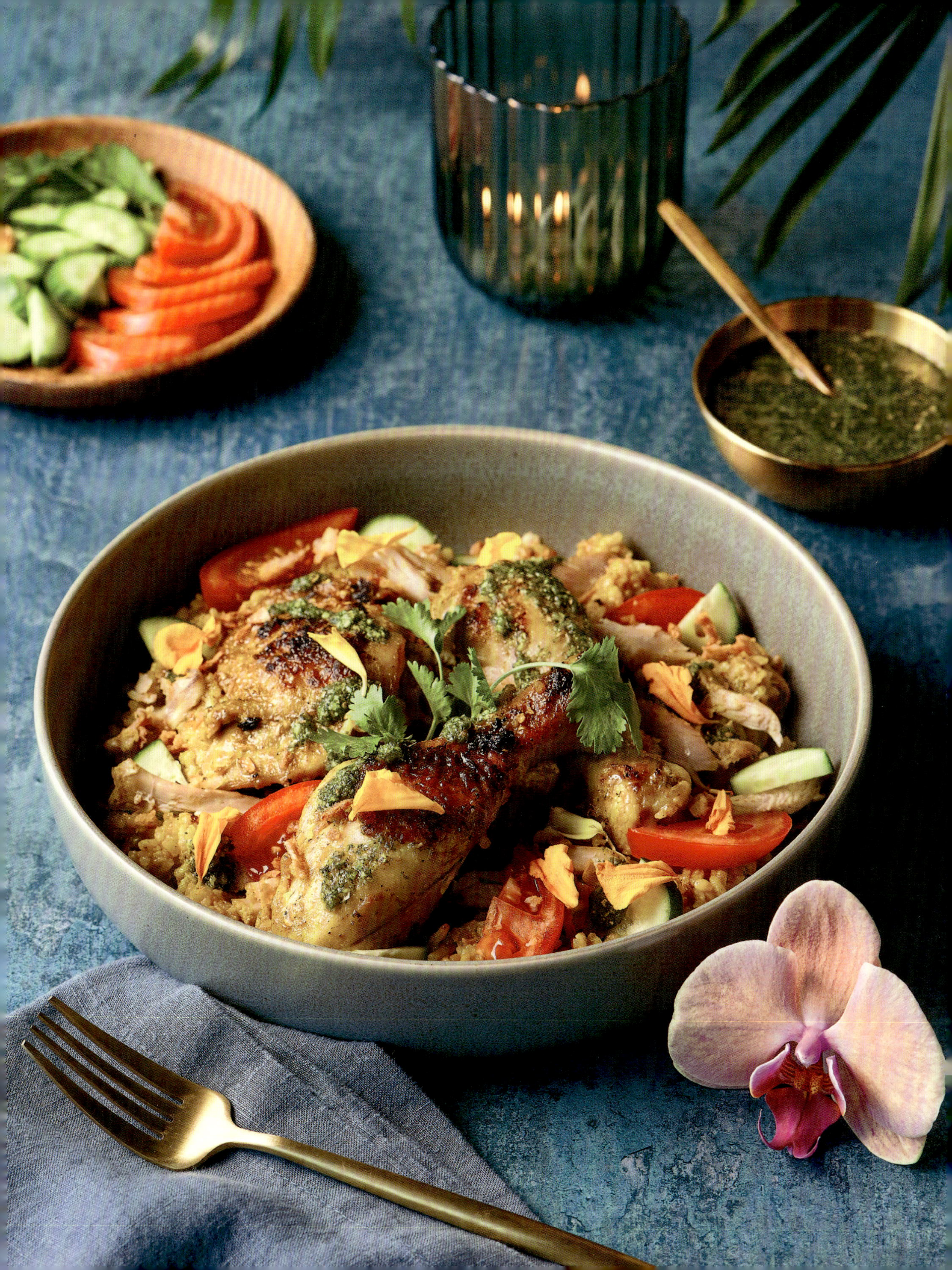

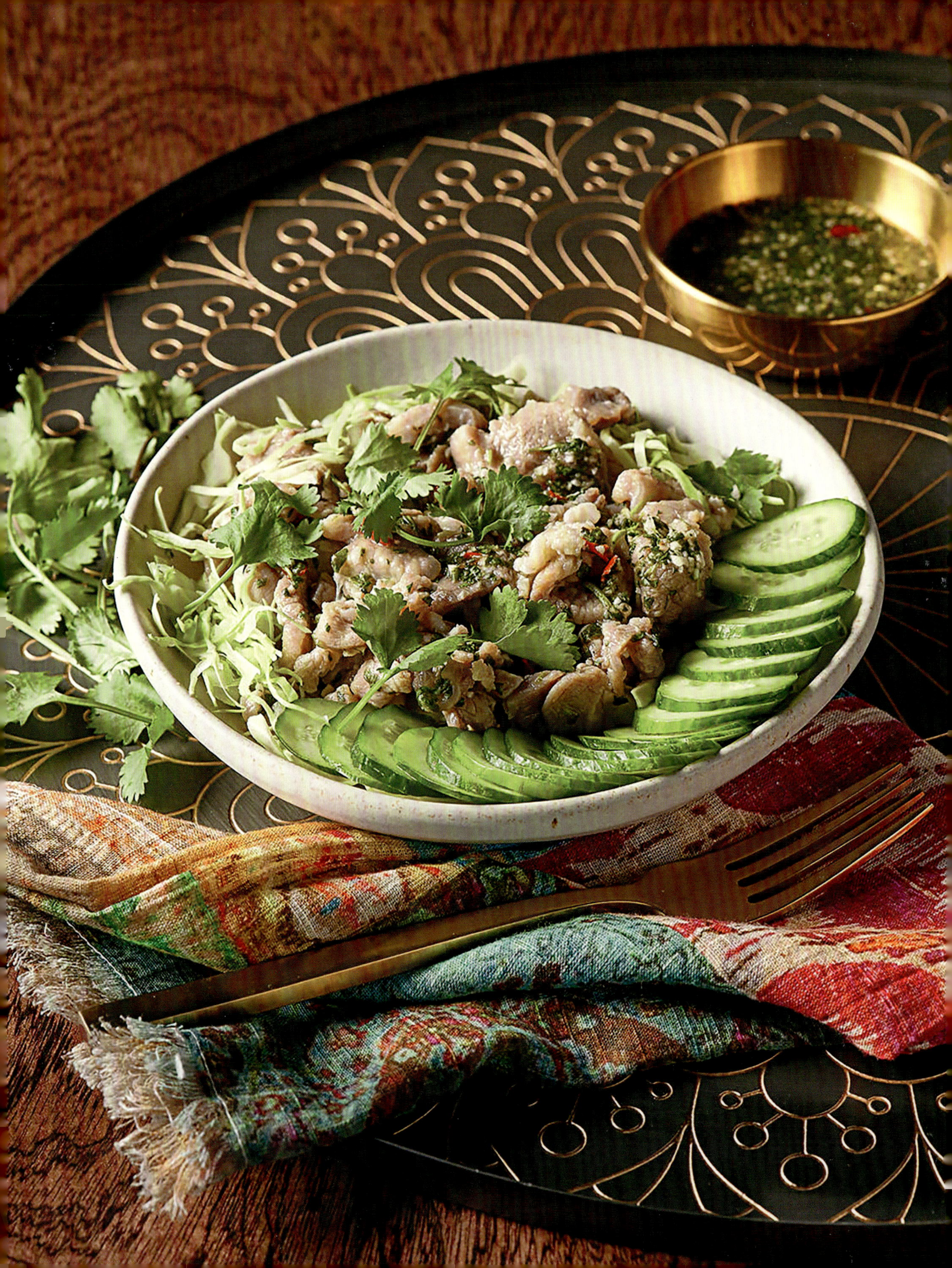

YIELD:
SERVES 4 TO 6

TIME:
25 MINUTES, PLUS 1 HOUR MARINATING

- 1 pound boneless pork shoulder
- 2 tablespoons Thai soy sauce
- 2 tablespoons cornstarch
- ¼ cup water
- 1 tablespoon vegetable or other neutral oil
- 1 teaspoon baking soda
- 5 cloves garlic, peeled
- 2 Thai chiles, stemmed
- ¼ cup palm sugar (see Note, page 96)
- ½ cup fresh lime juice
- ½ bunch cilantro (leaves and tender stems only)
- 4 to 6 cups shredded cabbage
- 4 to 6 Persian cucumbers, thinly sliced on a bias

Special Equipment
Food processor

Lime Pork (Moo Manao)

Silk, cotton, linen. A true luxury experience begins with texture. We think it's fitting that the key to making the pork in this dish super tender is a technique called "velveting." This requires the pork to rest soundly in a rub or marinade made with cornstarch. A small amount of baking soda also helps tenderize the meat and is especially crucial given the meat is allotted such a short cook time. The deeper flavor of this dish comes later, when you add the dressing, a delicious blend of garlic, chiles, palm sugar, and lime juice.

Freeze the pork shoulder on a cutting board for about 20 minutes, or until firm but not completely frozen. Slice thinly against the grain. Transfer to a large bowl.

In a small bowl, whisk together the soy sauce and cornstarch. Whisk in the water, oil, and baking soda. Pour over the pork and toss to coat. Cover and refrigerate for 1 hour.

In the bowl of a food processor, combine the garlic, chiles, palm sugar, lime juice, and cilantro. Pulse until finely chopped. Transfer to a large heatproof bowl.

Bring a medium pot of water to a boil over high heat. Working in batches, add the pork to the pot and boil until cooked through, 2 to 4 minutes. Use a wire skimmer to transfer the cooked pork to the bowl with the dressing (make sure the pork is well drained, so that the dressing doesn't become watered down). Repeat with all of the pork. Toss to coat in the dressing.

Divide the cabbage among four to six wide, shallow bowls. Top with the cooked pork, spooning any dressing left in the bowl over the top of the pork. Arrange the cucumber slices around the outside of the cabbage and serve.

THAILAND — EVENING SERVICE

YIELD:
SERVES 4
TIME:
30 MINUTES
GF

Sauce
⅓ cup palm sugar (see Note, page 96)
⅓ cup water
¼ cup tamarind paste
⅓ cup fish sauce

Pad Thai
8 ounces rice noodles
4 tablespoons vegetable or other neutral oil
1 pound medium shrimp, peeled, deveined, and tails removed
4 cloves garlic, chopped
2 medium shallots, thinly sliced
8 ounces firm tofu, drained and diced
4 large eggs, lightly beaten
2 cups bean sprouts
½ cup roasted, unsalted peanuts, chopped
Lime wedges, for serving

Special Equipment
Wok

Pad Thai Goong

Much like Satay (page 107), pad Thai has gained popularity all over the world. A particularly recent recipe, in the grand scheme of things, it was created specifically to serve as the national dish. The key to a good Pad Thai Goong is in the sauce. We consider it imperative to use true palm sugar rather than coconut sugar here. If you'd prefer not to source this yourself, well, know that you can count on us to use palm sugar when we prepare this dish for you during your next stay.

To make the sauce: In a small saucepan over medium heat, combine the palm sugar and water. Stir until the sugar has dissolved. Remove from the heat, then stir in the tamarind paste and fish sauce.

To make the pad Thai: Bring a large pot of water to a boil over high heat. Cook the rice noodles according to the package instructions (a shorter cook time is best, because the noodles will cook more and absorb additional liquid later in the preparation). Drain the noodles and set aside.

While the noodles are cooking, heat 2 tablespoons of the oil in a large wok over high heat. Cook the shrimp in two batches, tossing constantly until just cooked through, 2 to 3 minutes. Transfer to a large bowl.

Heat the remaining 2 tablespoons of oil in the wok. Add the garlic and shallots and cook, moving them constantly, until fragrant, about 30 seconds. Add the tofu and cook, tossing until warmed through, 2 to 3 minutes.

Push the tofu, garlic, and shallots to one side of the wok. Pour the eggs into the bottom of the wok and cook, stirring constantly, until they are barely dry. Move them to the side with the garlic, shallots, and tofu.

Add the cooked shrimp, bean sprouts, half the peanuts, and the cooked noodles to the wok. Toss until well mixed. Add the sauce and cook until it's just absorbed.

Divide the pad Thai among four bowls and top with the remaining peanuts. Serve immediately with lime wedges.

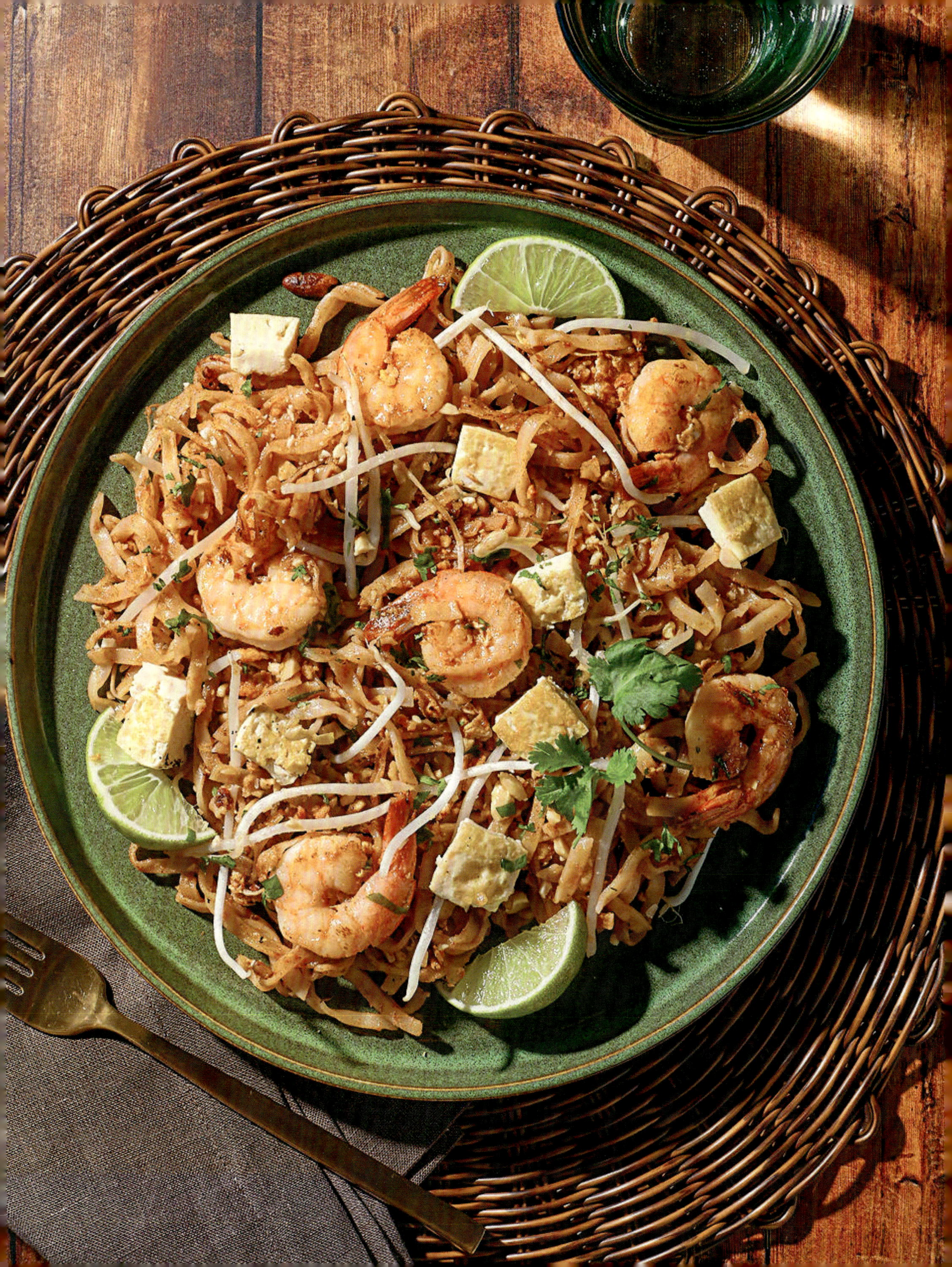

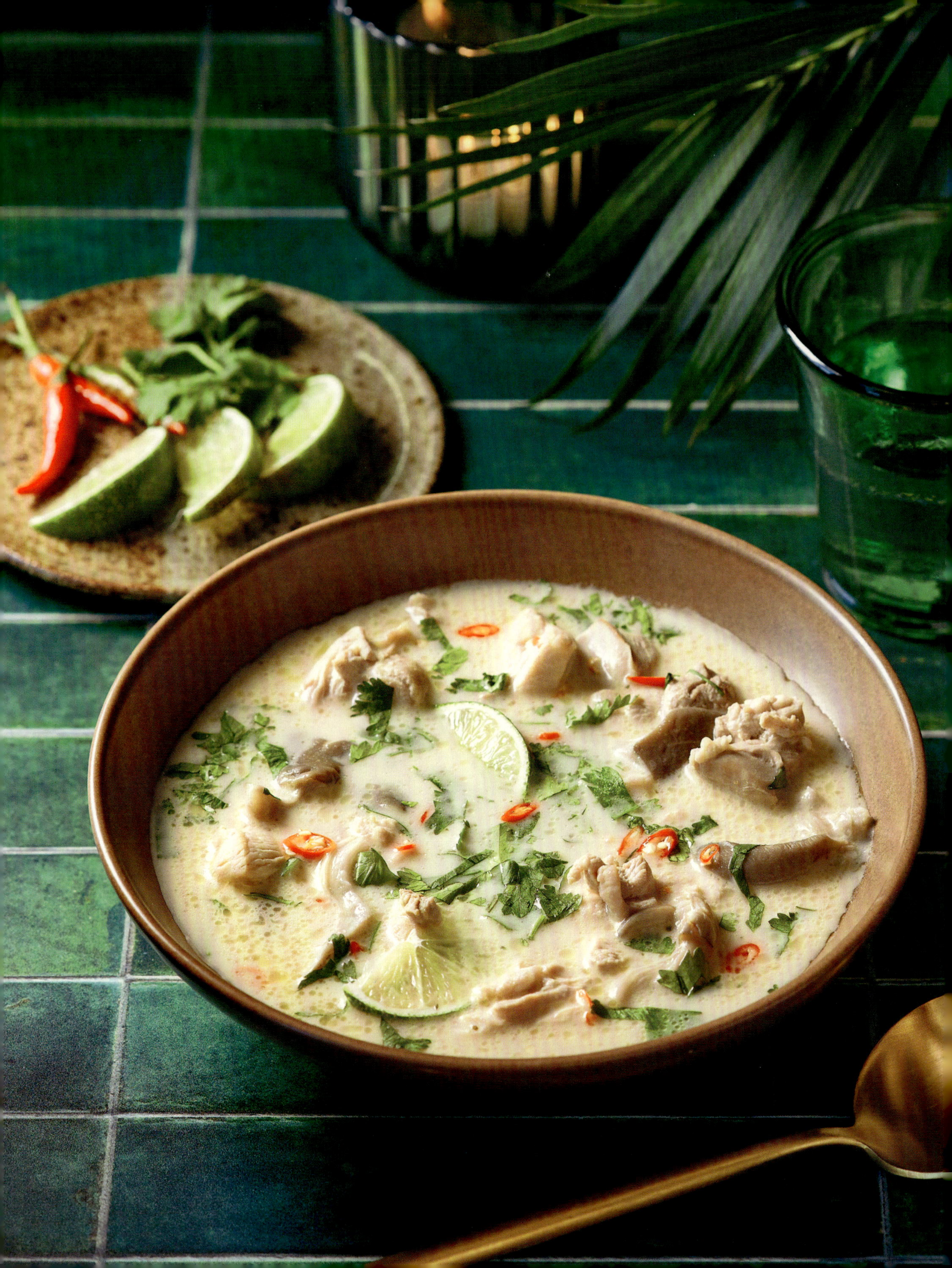

YIELD:
SERVES 4
TIME:
30 MINUTES
GF

3 cups chicken stock

3 stalks lemongrass (bottom halves only), smashed and cut to 1-inch pieces

4-inch piece galangal, thinly sliced

10 makrut lime leaves, torn and lightly crushed

One 13.5-ounce can coconut milk

2 Thai chiles, thinly sliced

8 ounces oyster mushrooms, torn into 1- to 2-inch pieces

1 pound boneless, skinless chicken thighs, cut into 1-inch chunks

2 teaspoons palm sugar (see Note, page 96)

2 tablespoons fish sauce, plus more if needed

¼ cup fresh lime juice

For Serving
Chopped cilantro

Lime wedges

Cooked jasmine rice (optional)

Special Equipment
Dutch oven (optional)

Tom Kha Gai

When you're looking to impress, but without breaking that relaxing vacation spell, we strongly recommend Tom Kha Gai. This soup tastes as though it took hours to make, but it manages to collect mountains of flavor in a mere 30 minutes. Enjoy as a starter or with a heaping helping of fragrant jasmine rice to have as a meal. We feel confident you'll get the adulation you deserve without breaking a sweat.

In a Dutch oven or medium pot, combine the chicken stock, lemongrass, galangal, and lime leaves. Bring to a boil over high heat, and then decrease to a simmer. Simmer for 15 minutes. Strain out the lemongrass, galangal, and lime leaves, reserving the liquid and discarding the solids.

Return the liquid to the Dutch oven or pot. Add the coconut milk and Thai chiles. Bring to a boil, and then stir in the mushrooms. Decrease to a simmer and cook until the mushrooms are tender, about 3 minutes. Add the chicken, palm sugar, fish sauce, and lime juice. Stir to combine and simmer until the chicken is completely cooked through, 3 to 5 minutes. Taste and add fish sauce, if needed.

Divide the soup among four bowls and serve with the cilantro, lime wedges, and rice (if desired).

YIELD:
SERVES 4

TIME:
1 HOUR

GF

"Rainbow" Rice Salad (Khao Yum)

Rice
2 cups jasmine rice
¼ teaspoon butterfly pea powder

Dressing
1 small shallot, coarsely chopped
2 cloves garlic, peeled
4-inch piece lemongrass (bottom half, hard outer leaves removed)
1-inch piece ginger, sliced
¼ cup water
¼ cup palm sugar (see Note, page 96)
3 tablespoons fish sauce
1 tablespoon Thai soy sauce
1 tablespoon tamarind paste

Salad
1 cup shredded red cabbage
1 cup shredded white or green cabbage
½ cup kaffir lime leaves or Thai basil, shredded
1 pomelo or large grapefruit, supremed (see page 56)
1 mango, peeled, pitted, and thinly sliced
2 medium carrots, peeled and julienned
4 Persian cucumbers, thinly sliced on a bias
½ cup shredded coconut, toasted
2 cups bean sprouts

Special Equipment
Rice cooker
Blender or food processor

This is a dish that changes from person to person, season to season, day to day. It is a Southern Thai specialty that has become popular throughout the country due, perhaps, to some Instagram-worthy preparations. While Khao Yum is infinitely customizable, one of the few criteria is that you must start with rice. While dyeing said rice *is* optional, good presentation, however you define it, is another nonnegotiable. The adage about "eating with our eyes" exists for a reason, after all. We'd advise that the key to a beautiful salad is less about adhering to a strict list of ingredients and more about including as many colors of the rainbow as you can. Our recipe includes many ingredients commonly found in Khao Yum, but what you do with this list is entirely up to you! If that includes posting your creation online, our chefs *would* appreciate a mention, though.

To make the rice: Place the rice in a mixing bowl and add enough water to cover. Swish the rice vigorously with your hand for about a minute. Drain the water. Repeat four or five times, or until the water runs clear.

In a rice cooker, combine the rice, butterfly pea powder, and water to the 2-cup mark. Cook the rice according to the manufacturer's instructions.

To make the dressing: In a blender or food processor, combine the shallot, garlic, lemongrass, ginger, water, palm sugar, fish sauce, soy sauce, and tamarind paste. Blend until smooth. Transfer to a cruet or small pitcher and set aside.

To assemble the salad: Lightly moisten the inside of a 1-cup rice bowl or measuring cup. Pack the bowl full of rice, compress it, and overturn onto the center of a plate. Repeat with the remaining rice to make four plates.

Divide the cabbages, lime leaves, pomelo segments, mango, carrots, cucumbers, toasted coconut, and bean sprouts evenly among the plates. Arrange each element in small piles around the rice. Serve with the dressing on the side.

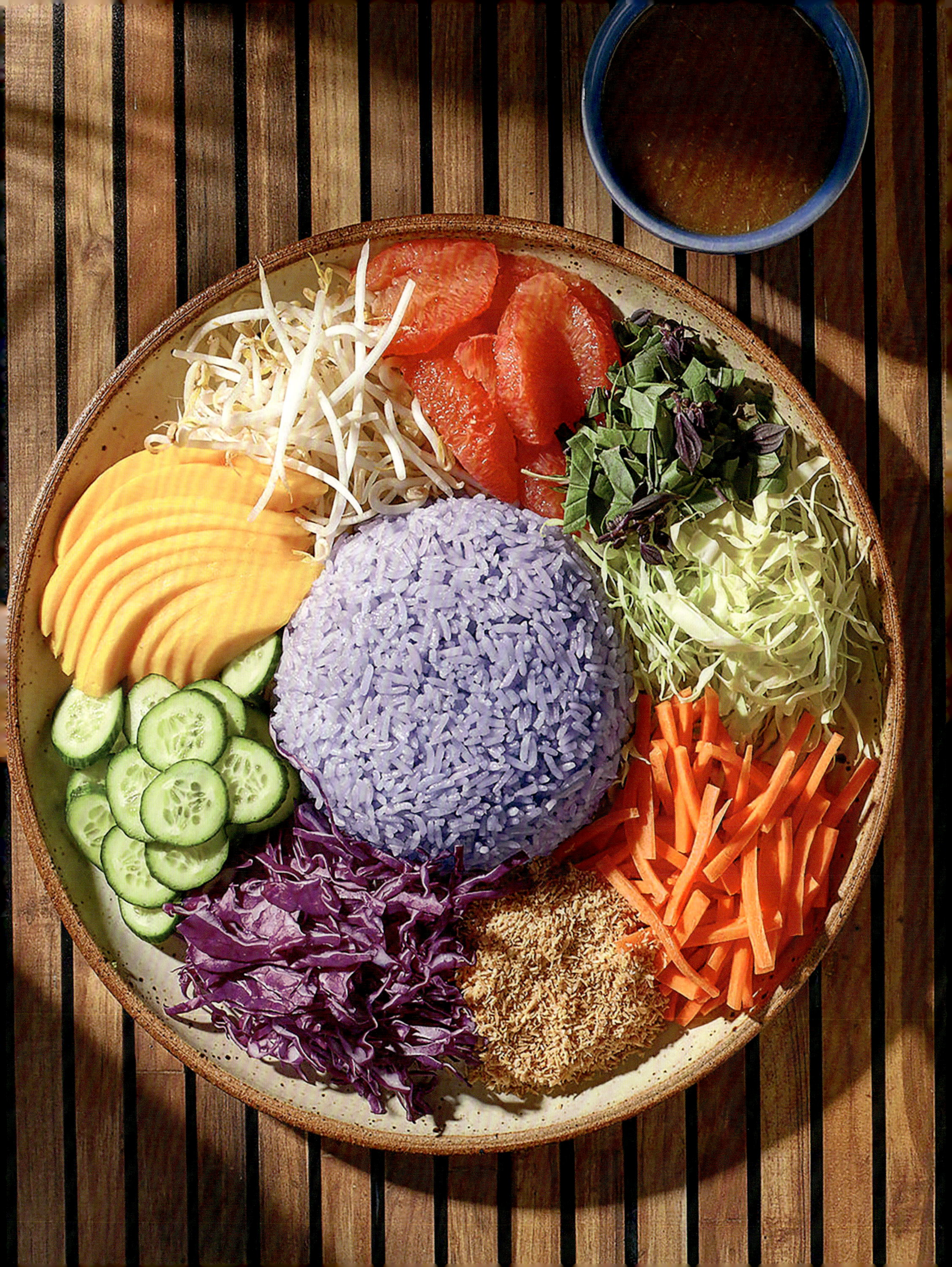

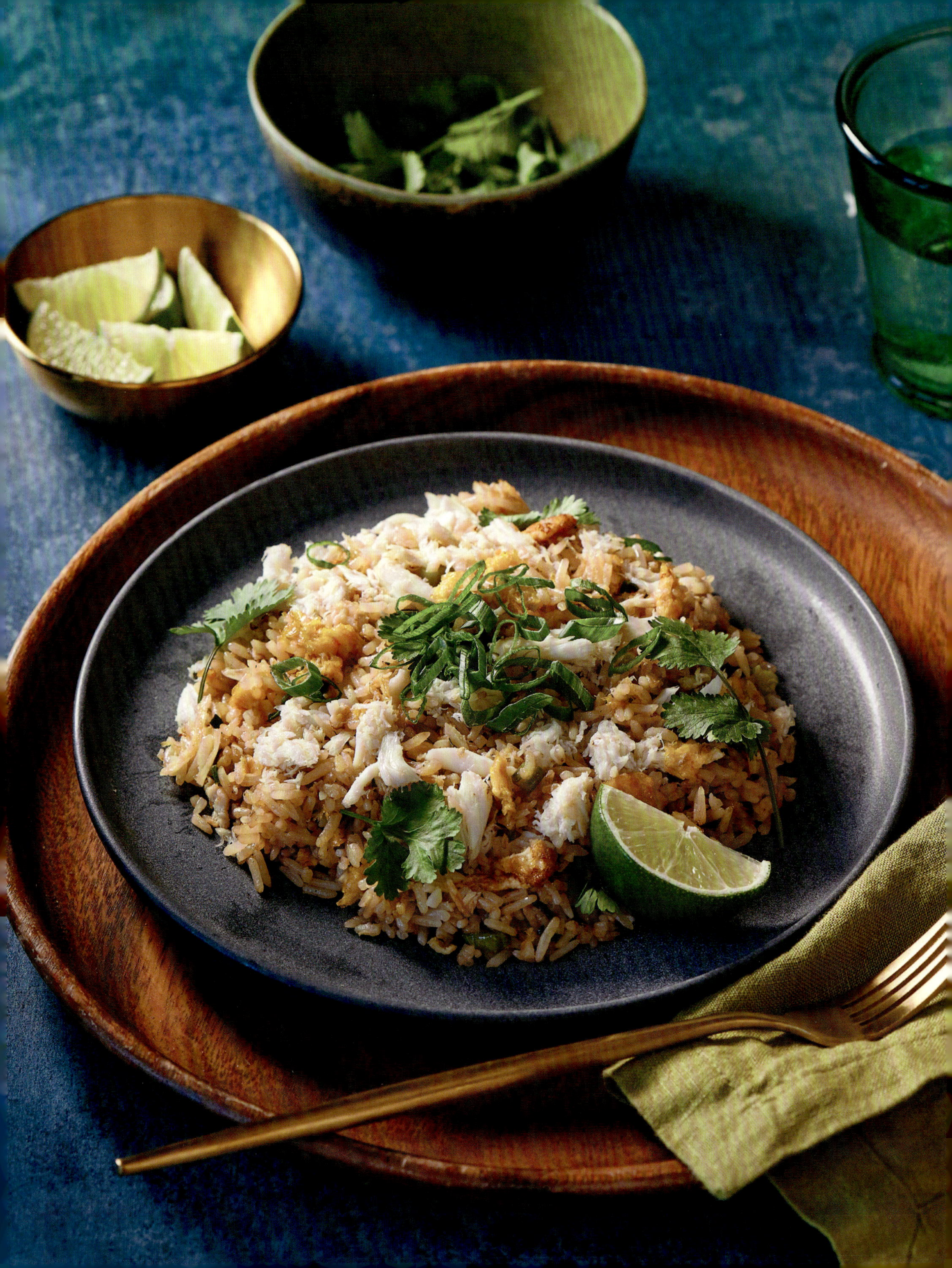

YIELD: SERVES 4

TIME: 30 MINUTES

- 4 cups cooked jasmine rice, preferably day old
- 4 tablespoons vegetable or other neutral oil, plus more if needed
- 3 large eggs
- 6 cloves garlic, chopped
- 3 scallions, thinly sliced
- 8 ounces cooked crabmeat
- 3 tablespoons Thai soy sauce, plus more as needed
- 1 tablespoon fish sauce, plus more as needed
- Chopped cilantro, for garnish
- Lime wedges, for serving

Special Equipment
Wok, or large deep pan

Crab Fried Rice (Khao Phat Poo)

The seemingly endless varieties of fried rice around the world frankly outnumber The White Lotus properties. So, we can't claim to offer recipes encompassing each region's approach. The protein choices alone range from chicken to shrimp to pork to beef to eggs or tofu. There's even a khao phat Amerikan, which participants in our history-geared activities may recall was created in an attempt to appeal to American soldiers' palates. It's been known to incorporate fried chicken and even ketchup. Our own Khao Phat Poo takes an entirely different approach. It includes little more than sweet, succulent crabmeat. It's simple, elegant, and one of our most popular dishes. If you prepare this at home, you'll be certain to impress.

Let the rice come to room temperature (this will prevent the wok temperature from lowering too much during cooking). If it's easier, microwave the rice just enough to warm it through.

Heat 2 tablespoons of the oil in a large wok over high heat until it shimmers. Add half the rice and cook, tossing constantly, until just beginning to turn crispy and smell toasty. Transfer to a bowl and repeat with the remaining 2 tablespoons of oil and rice. Transfer the second batch of rice to the same bowl as the first.

If the wok is dry, add another tablespoon of oil. Add the eggs and cook, stirring frequently, until they are just set, then push them to the side. Add the garlic and scallions and cook, stirring constantly, until fragrant, about 1 minute.

Return the rice to the wok. Mix it with all the ingredients until completely combined. Push the rice to the sides, leaving space in the center. Add the crabmeat and cook for about 1 minute, or until it is just beginning to crisp on the bottom. Toss with the rice until combined.

Push all the rice to the center. Drizzle the soy sauce and fish sauce down the sides, so that they drip into the rice (this caramelizes the sauces slightly, enhancing the flavors). Toss until the soy and fish sauces have been absorbed and are well distributed. Taste and add soy sauce or fish sauce as needed.

Transfer to a large serving bowl. Garnish with chopped cilantro and serve with lime wedges.

THAILAND – EVENING SERVICE

YIELD:
SERVES 4 TO 6

TIME:
40 MINUTES

GF

Crispy Pork
1 pound pork belly
6 cups water
¼ cup kosher salt
2 tablespoons white vinegar
2 cups vegetable or other neutral oil

For Serving
Thai jasmine rice or sticky rice
Sriracha
Lime wedges

Special Equipment
Dutch oven
Cooking thermometer

Crispy Pork (Moo Krop)

We believe that when you're on vacation, you should be able to take your time. However, that time shouldn't be taken up waiting to eat. Knowing that the key to a crispy pork belly dish is usually a long, slow roast, our chefs determined to achieve similar results by triple-cooking smaller pieces of pork belly. They start by simmering the pork in a solution of vinegar and salt, followed by frying in oil once at a low temperature, and then again at a high temperature. They even reuse the same pot at each stage. Trust us when we say that 40 minutes is all you need for tender pork belly with shatteringly crisp skin. So, if you're having Moo Krop with us, you won't be waiting long, whether you're dining at our restaurant or ordering room service.

To make the crispy pork: Cut the pork belly into strips about 6 inches long by 1½ inches thick and transfer to a Dutch oven. Add the water, salt, and vinegar. Bring to a boil over high heat, then decrease to a simmer. Cook for 15 minutes. Transfer to a wire rack.

Discard the cooking liquid, wipe out the Dutch oven, and return to the stove over low heat. Make sure the Dutch oven is completely dry before adding the oil.

Add the oil and heat to 325°F over medium heat. Pat the pork belly completely dry with paper towels. Fry it for 10 to 15 minutes, turning occasionally, until it starts to firm up and turn lightly golden.

Transfer the pork back to the wire rack. Increase the oil heat to 375°F. Return the pork to the oil. Fry, turning occasionally, until completely firm, the skin bubbles, and the surface of the pork is a deep golden brown, 4 to 6 minutes. Transfer to the wire rack to cool until just warm.

Serve with jasmine rice, sriracha, and lime wedges.

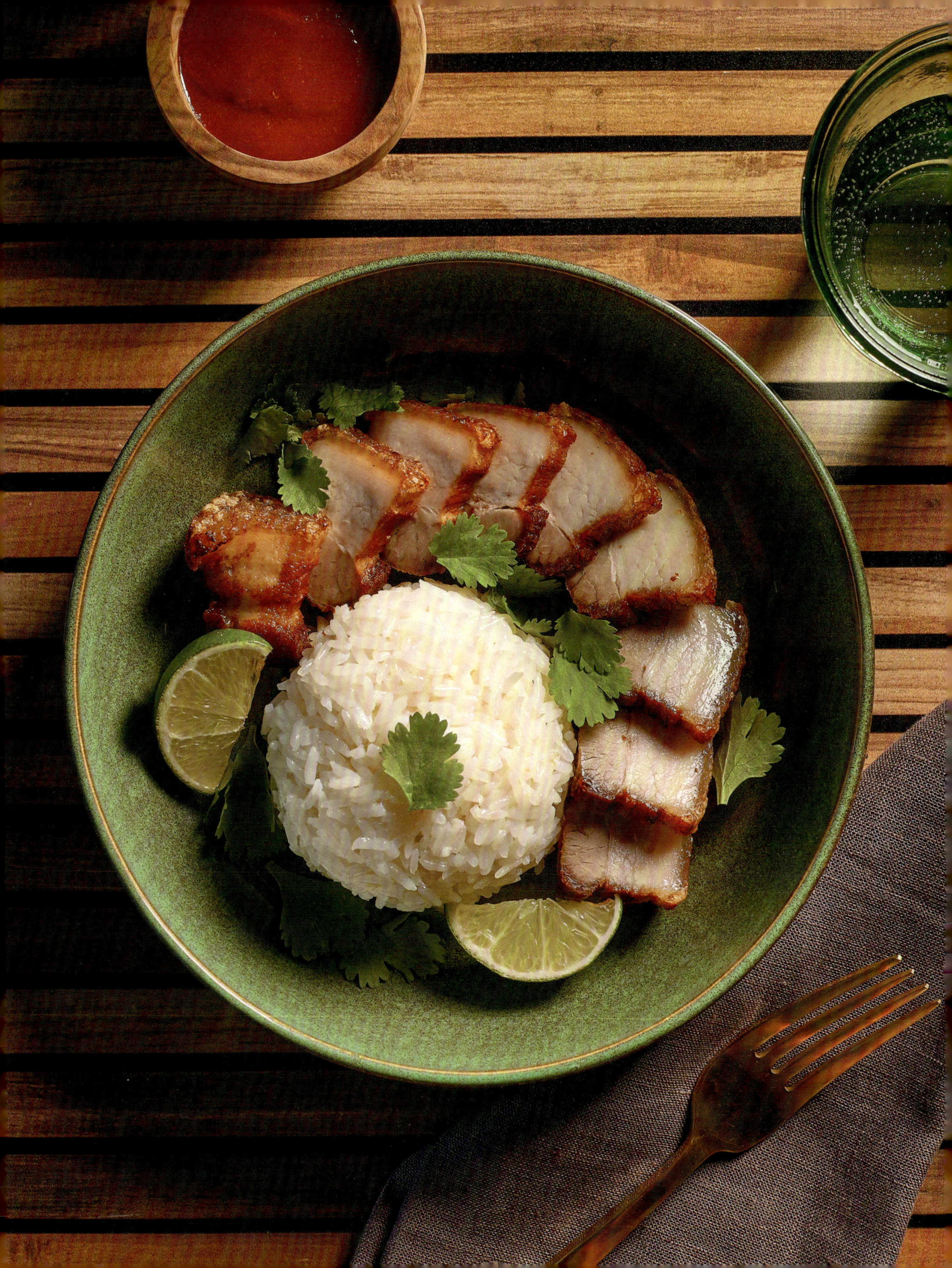

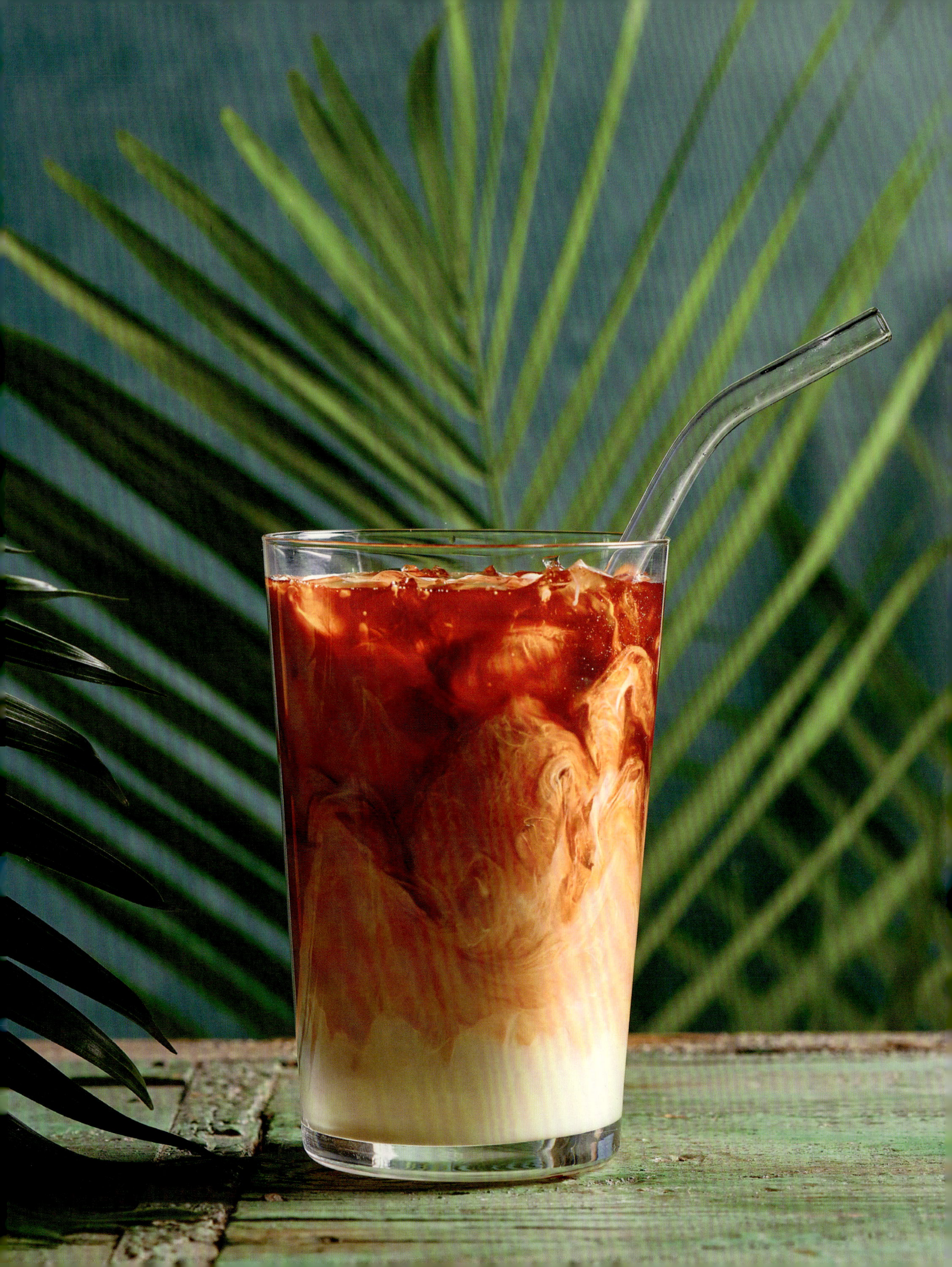

YIELD:
SERVES 4

TIME:
10 MINUTES, PLUS
3 HOURS CHILLING

GF, V

4 cups water
½ cup Thai tea blend
½ cup condensed milk
½ cup evaporated milk

Thai Iced Tea

It may surprise you to know that Thai tea gets its signature orange look not from the tea itself, nor from some blend of spices, but from food coloring. The iconic flavor comes from strong black tea and a hint of vanilla. Despite our chefs' best efforts to reinterpret this drink—and they're some of the best in the world—there was just no comparing to the commercially available blends that many locals use in their own homes. Sometimes, there's just no outdoing what already works. And to quote something you may have heard wisely spoken around these walls, "Nothing comes from nothing."

In a medium saucepan over high heat, bring the water to a boil. Stir in the tea and remove from the heat. Let steep for 3 to 5 minutes. Strain out the leaves and transfer to a heatproof container. Refrigerate for at least 3 hours, and up to 5 days.

When ready to serve, pour 2 tablespoons of condensed milk into four 16-ounce glasses. Top with ice, and then add the tea, pouring slowly. Carefully top each glass with 2 tablespoons of evaporated milk and serve.

YIELD: MAKES 6

TIME: 1 HOUR, PLUS UP TO 26 HOURS RESTING

V

- 1½ cups all-purpose flour
- 1½ teaspoons vegetable or other neutral oil, plus more as needed
- 1 teaspoon kosher salt
- 2 teaspoons sugar
- 1 large egg
- 2 tablespoons unsalted butter, softened (or nondairy substitute)
- 3 tablespoons milk (or nondairy substitute, such as almond milk or oat milk)
- 6 small bananas, peeled and cut crosswise into ½-inch-thick slices
- ½ cup sweetened condensed milk or condensed coconut milk

Special Equipment
Stand mixer with dough hook attachment

Banana Pancakes (Roti Pisang)

You'll find these tender, flaky pastries filled with fresh banana and drizzled with sweetened, condensed milk sold at food stalls throughout Thailand. Our version starts with our own Roti dough (page 99), which gives the treat its buttery, slightly salty crust. Between the natural sweetness of the bananas and the extra burst of sticky sweetness from the condensed milk, Roti Pisang works well as either a midday snack or dessert. For our dairy-free guests, we offer an equally delicious alternative, swapping in plant-based butter and milk for the dough and a drizzle of sweetened condensed coconut milk on top—the latter pairs so beautifully with the bananas that you may choose to use it regardless of dietary needs. Either way, you'll be biting into a moment of sweet self-care and making new memories.

In the bowl of a stand mixer fitted with the dough hook attachment, combine the flour, oil, salt, sugar, egg, butter, and milk. Mix on low speed just until the flour is moistened. Increase the speed to medium and mix until the dough is smooth and elastic, about 10 minutes.

Oil a large bowl. Transfer the dough to the bowl and roll it around until completely coated in oil. Cover and refrigerate for 4 hours, and up to 24 hours.

When you're ready to make the roti, let the dough come to room temperature for 2 hours. Divide it into 6 equal portions.

Place one piece of dough on a well-oiled work surface. Coat it with more oil and use the palm of your hand to flatten the dough as thin as possible. (You should be able to see the work surface through much of the dough.) By the time you're done, the dough should be almost paper-thin. Don't worry if it tears in places.

Coat the bottom of a nonstick skillet with vegetable oil. Heat over medium heat until the oil shimmers. Working quickly, lay a dough portion in the pan and cover the center with banana slices (you won't use all the banana in preparing the roti; reserve some for garnish). Fold the outer edges of the dough over the bananas to create a square packet, then press the dough down with a flat spatula to ensure even contact on the pan. Fry for 3 to 5 minutes, or until deep golden brown and crisp. Flip and fry on the other side for 3 to 5 minutes more. Transfer to a wire rack to cool. Repeat with the remaining dough pieces and bananas.

Place each roti on a plate, drizzle with 2 tablespoons of the condensed milk, and garnish with the remaining banana slices.

NOTE

When selecting bananas, choose ones that are just barely ripe with a little green on the peel. If your bananas are too ripe, they'll turn to mush as the roti cooks.

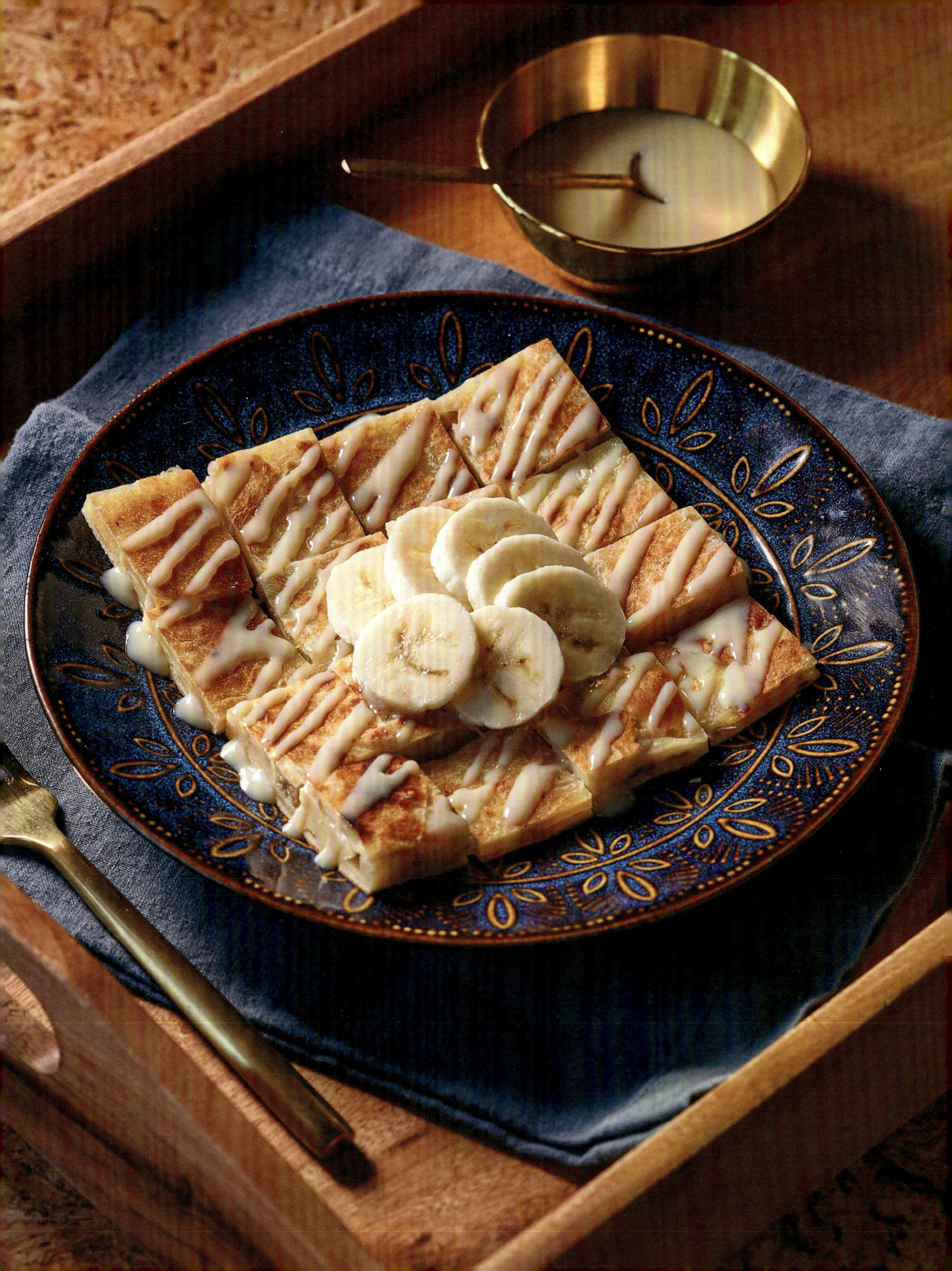

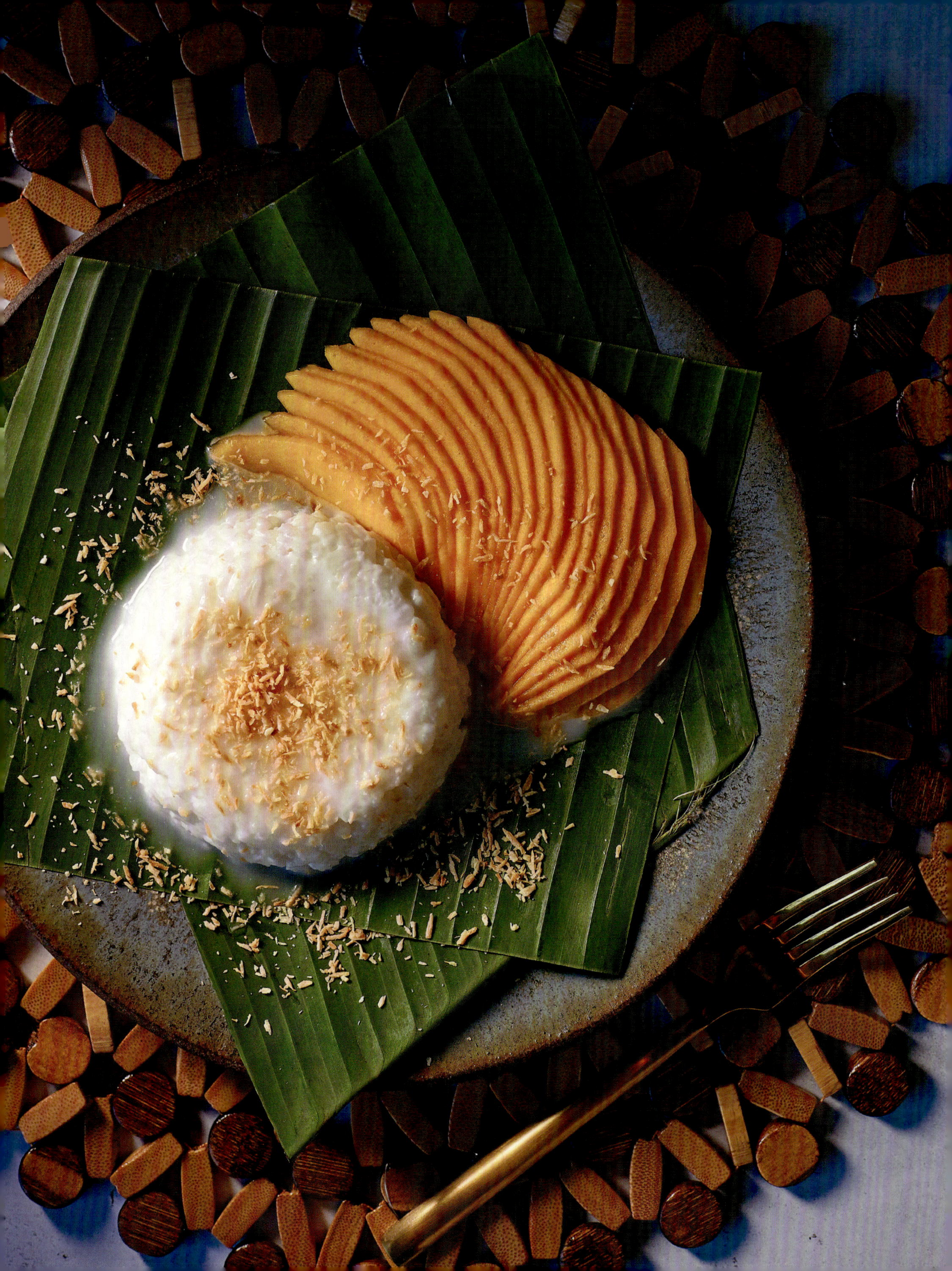

YIELD:
SERVES 4

TIME:
1 HOUR, PLUS 4 TO 24 HOURS SOAKING

GF, V+

---

1 cup Thai sweet sticky rice

One 13.5-ounce can coconut milk (see Note)

½ cup plus 2 tablespoons sugar

¾ teaspoon kosher salt

1 teaspoon tapioca starch or 2 teaspoons cornstarch

2 ripe mangoes, peeled, pitted, and sliced (preferably Ataulfo; see Note)

¼ cup shredded coconut, toasted

Special Equipment
Bamboo steamer
Cheesecloth
Wok

Sticky Rice and Mango

Is there a more classic Thai dessert than sticky rice with mango? We'll let you decide once you've tried ours. Just remember that a meal among familiar faces with the "usual" dishes can be transformed by a special setting. The rice sourced for this sticky, mango delight may be labeled "Thai Sticky Rice," "Thai Glutinous White Rice," or even "Thai Sweet Rice," but it's not inherently sweeter than other varieties of rice. It does, however, *become* sweet under the right circumstances. That's where we come in. Whether you're cooking our recipes at home or letting us put it all together, we'll bring the *right* touches for an unforgettable evening.

In a large mixing bowl, combine the rice and enough water to cover. Swish the rice vigorously with your hands for about 1 minute. Drain the water. Repeat four or five times, or until the water runs clear.

Cover the rice with 2 inches of water. Cover and let sit at room temperature for a least 4 hours, and up to 24 hours.

Drain the rice. Line a bamboo steamer basket with enough cheesecloth to fully wrap the rice. (You can also use a sheet of clean muslin or a thin, clean tea towel.) Transfer the rice to the steamer basket.

Add 2 inches of water to a wok and bring to a boil over high heat. Place the steamer basket over the water and steam the rice for 15 to 25 minutes, or until tender.

While the rice cooks, add 1 cup of the coconut milk to a small saucepan. Add ½ cup of the sugar and ½ teaspoon of the kosher salt. Bring to a simmer over medium-high heat, stirring until the sugar and salt have dissolved. Decrease the heat to a gentle simmer and cook until the rice is ready. It's okay if the mixture reduces a little bit.

Transfer the rice to a metal mixing bowl. Add the milk mixture and gently stir until completely combined. Cover and let sit for 15 minutes. Gently fold the rice with a rubber spatula, then cover and let sit for 15 minutes more, or until all of the liquid has been absorbed.

In a small saucepan, combine the remaining 2 tablespoons of sugar, the remaining ¼ teaspoon of salt, and the tapioca starch. Whisk until combined and no clumps of starch remain. Whisk in the remaining coconut milk. Cook over medium heat, whisking constantly, until the mixture comes to a simmer. Whisk for 1 minute more, then remove from the heat.

Divide the rice among four small plates or wide, shallow bowls. Mound it to one side. Arrange sliced mango beside each rice mound and drizzle with the coconut milk sauce. Sprinkle with 1 tablespoon of the toasted coconut and serve.

NOTE

It's important that the coconut milk be well blended. The cream in canned coconut milk has a tendency to rise and solidify. If this is the case, add all of the coconut milk to a blender and blend on high speed for 1 to 2 minutes until uniform before using it in this recipe. When selecting mangoes, opt for Ataulfo mangoes, which are small with bright yellow skin. These are sometimes marketed and sold as "Yellow Mangoes" or "Champagne Mangoes"—they are sweeter, more tender, and closer in flavor and texture to those served in Thailand.

DIETARY CONSIDERATIONS

KEY

V = Vegetarian   V* = Easily Made Vegetarian   V+ = Vegan
V+* = Easily Made Vegan   GF = Gluten free   GF*= Easily Made Gluten free

Chapter 1: Maui

MORNING SERVICE

Tropical Sunrise Smoothie .... GF, V+
Loco Moco
Coconut French Toast V
Ricotta Soufflé Pancakes V
Malasadas V
Spam Musubi
Lomi Lomi Salmon .... GF
Manapua
Garlic Shrimp
Poke Bowl

EVENING SERVICE

Coconut Seafood Chowder .... GF
Huli Huli Chicken
Seared Sesame-Crusted Mahi Mahi
Macadamia-Crusted Pork
Fish Tacos .... GF
Saimin
Seared Steak with Shiitake Mushrooms and Miso Butter
Macadamia Haupia Tart V
Coconut Cake V
Ube-Marbled Butter Mochi .... GF, V

Chapter 2: Sicily

MORNING SERVICE

Brioche col Tuppo V
Coffee Granita .... GF, V
Blood Orange and Fennel Salad .... GF, V
Warm Ricotta with Lemon and Olive Oil .... GF*, V
Bruschetta V
Caponata .... GF, V+*
Sfincione
Arancini

EVENING SERVICE

Pasta Pescatore
Panelle .... GF, V+
Pasta con Pesto alla Trapanese V
Pasta alla Norma V
Pasta con le Sarde
Braciole Messinesi
Pasta di Mandorla Cookies .... GF, V
Cannoli V
Gelato di Pistacchio .... GF, V
Lemon Prosecco Granita .... GF, V
Pignolata V
Cassata V

Chapter 3: Thailand

MORNING SERVICE

Rice Soup (Khao Tom Goong)
Rice Porridge (Jok)
Thai-Style Omelet (Khao Khai Chiao) .... GF, V
Roti V
Sour Curry (Kaeng Som) .... GF
Tom Yum Goong
Massaman Curry (Kaeng Massaman) .... GF
Satay
Nam Prik Goong Siap .... GF

EVENING SERVICE

Yellow Curry (Kaeng Kari) .... GF
Chicken Biryani (Khao Mok Gai) .... GF
Lime Pork (Moo Manao)
Pad Thai Goong .... GF
Tom Kha Gai .... GF
Rice Salad (Khao Yum) .... GF
Crab Fried Rice (Khao Phat Poo)
Crispy Pork (Moo Krop) .... GF
Thai Iced Tea .... GF, V
Banana Pancakes (Roti Pisang) V
Sticky Rice and Mango .... GF, V+

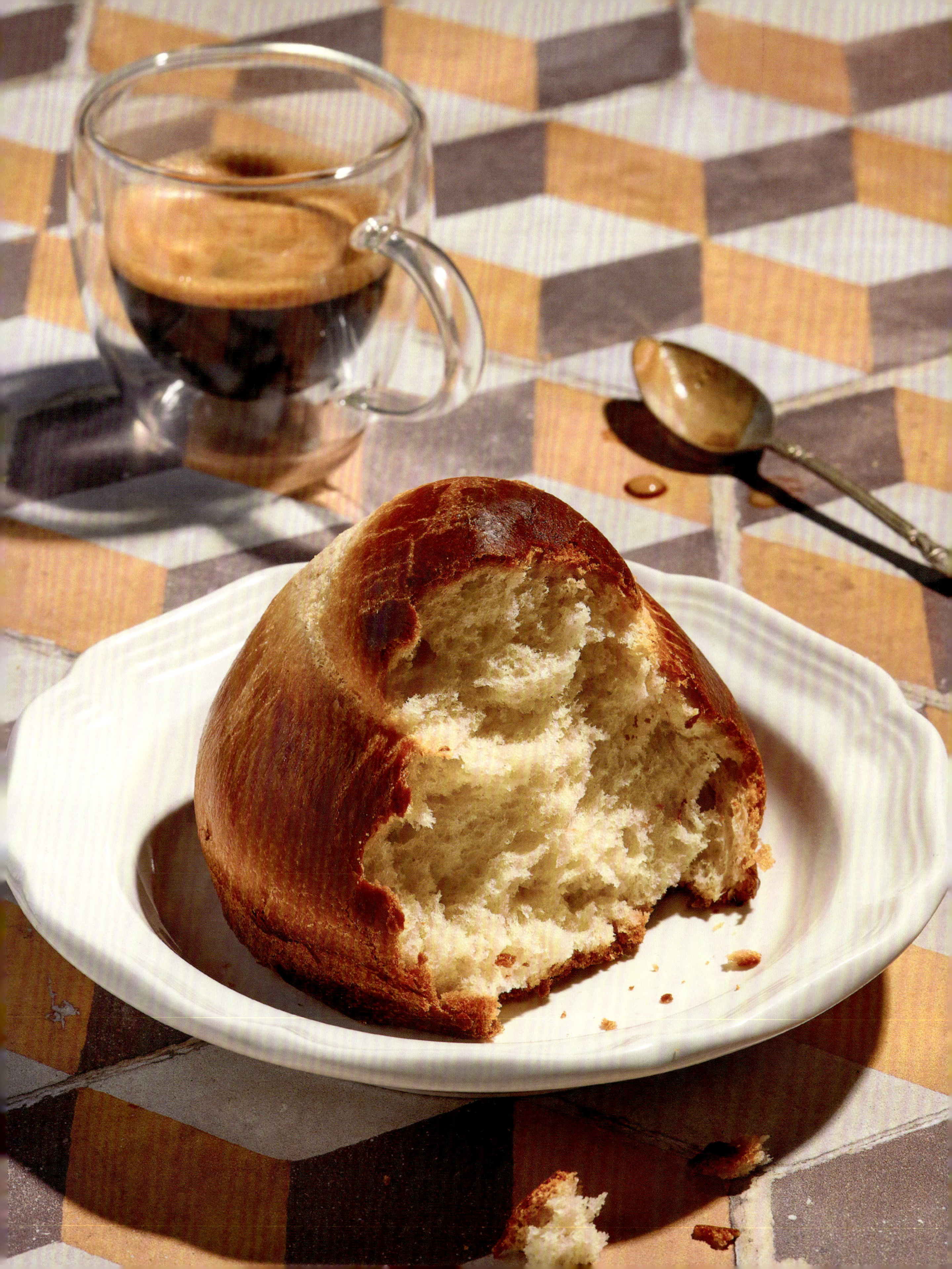

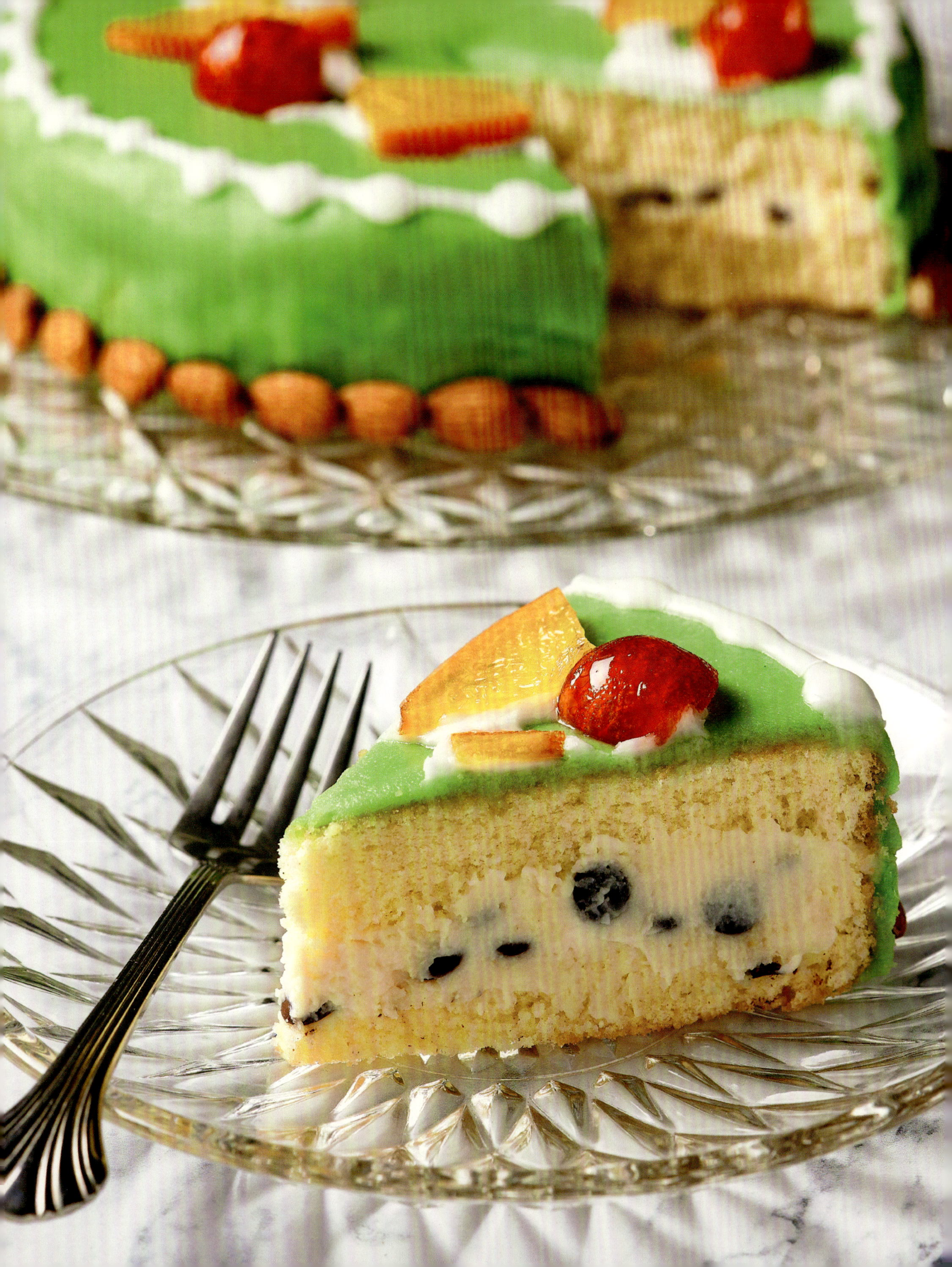

MEASUREMENT CONVERSIONS

KITCHEN MEASUREMENTS

CUP	TABLESPOON	TEASPOON	FLUID OUNCES
1/16 cup	1 tablespoon	3 teaspoons	1/2 fluid ounce
1/8 cup	2 tablespoons	6 teaspoons	1 fluid ounce
1/4 cup	4 tablespoons	12 teaspoons	2 fluid ounces
1/3 cup	5 1/3 tablespoons	16 teaspoons	2 2/3 fluid ounces
1/2 cup	8 tablespoons	24 teaspoons	4 fluid ounces
2/3 cup	10 2/3 tablespoons	32 teaspoons	5 1/3 fluid ounces
3/4 cup	12 tablespoons	36 teaspoons	6 fluid ounces
1 cup	16 tablespoons	48 teaspoons	8 fluid ounces

GALLON	QUART	PINT	CUP	FLUID OUNCES
1/16 gallon	1/4 quart	1/2 pint	1 cup	8 fluid ounces
1/8 gallon	1/2 quart	1 pint	2 cups	16 fluid ounces
1/4 gallon	1 quart	2 pints	4 cups	32 fluid ounces
1/2 gallon	2 quarts	4 pints	8 cups	64 fluid ounces
1 gallon	4 quarts	8 pints	16 cups	128 fluid ounces

OVEN TEMPERATURES

CELCIUS	FAHRENHEIT
93°C	200°F
107°C	225°F
121°C	250°F
135°C	275°F
149°C	300°F
163°C	325°F
177°C	350°F
191°C	375°F
204°C	400°F
218°C	425°F
232°C	450°F

WEIGHT

GRAMS	OUNCES
14 grams	1/2 ounce
28 grams	1 ounce
57 grams	2 ounces
85 grams	3 ounces
113 grams	4 ounces
142 grams	5 ounces
170 grams	6 ounces
283 grams	10 ounces
397 grams	14 ounces
454 grams	16 ounces
907 grams	32 ounces

LENGTH

IMPERIAL	METRIC
1 inch	2.54 centimeters
2 inches	5 centimeters
4 inches	10 centimeters
6 inches	15 centimeters
8 inches	20 centimeters
10 inches	25 centimeters
12 inches	30 centimeters

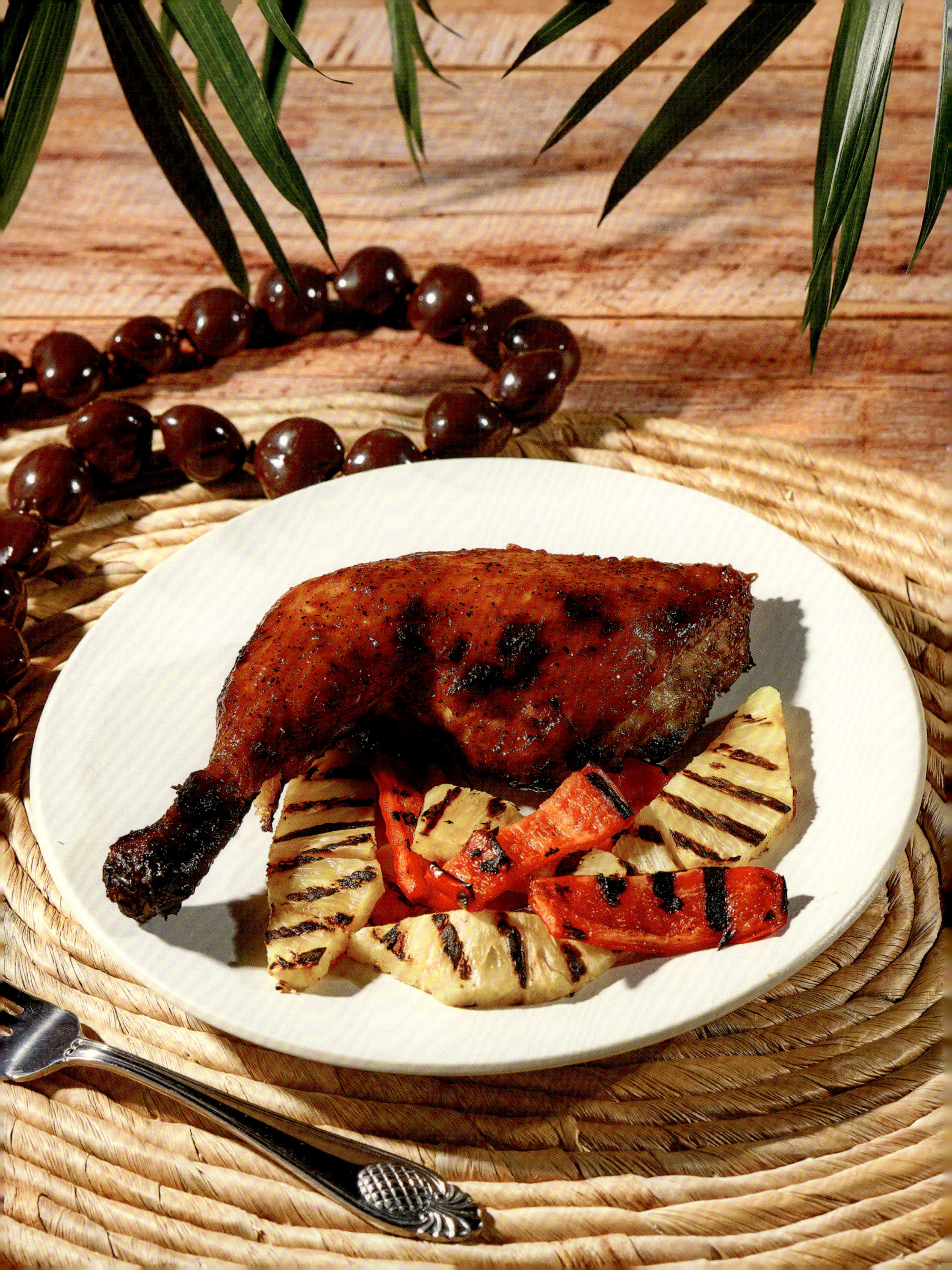

ABOUT THE AUTHOR

Jarrett Melendez is a GLAAD Media Award– and Eisner Award–nominated comic and graphic novel writer, cookbook author, and food journalist. He's best known for the award-winning graphic novel *Chef's Kiss*, a queer romance set in a restaurant, which he co-created with Danica Brine. The sequel, *Chef's Kiss Again*, will be released in 2026. Jarrett has also contributed to award-winning and nominated anthologies, including *Young Men in Love*, *All We Ever Wanted*, and *Young Men in Love 2: New Romances*. Jarrett is currently working on *Tales of the Fungo: The Legend of Cep*, to be published by Andrews McMeel; *Fujoshi Warriors*, an action comedy comic miniseries and love letter to both fujoshis and magical girl anime and manga; and a Webtoon.

As a cookbook author and food journalist, Jarrett has written countless articles and developed hundreds of original recipes that have appeared on *Bon Appétit*, *Epicurious*, *Saveur*, and Food52. He's written a total of seven cookbooks to date, including *My Pokémon Baking Book*, *RuneScape: The Official Cookbook*, *Percy Jackson and the Olympians: The Official Cookbook*, *The Official Wednesday Cookbook*, and *Eat the Borderlands*.

Jarrett grew up on the mean, deer-infested streets of Bucksport, Maine, but currently resides in Somerville, Massachusetts, with his collection of Monokuro Boo plush pigs.

ACKNOWLEDGMENTS

Thanks to my taste-testers: my roommate Emily, and Rosa, Vanessa, Emma, and the rest of the crew at Trina's Starlite Lounge. You all help me so much, and I appreciate you letting me off-load all the excess food when my fridge runs out of space. Appreciate you!

Thanks to Ray at Christina's Spice & Specialty Foods in Cambridge—you've always got all the spices and hard-to-find ingredients I need.

Thanks to the crew at Savenor's Butcher Shop—it's always a delight to come by and get meat, seafood, and pantry items.

And thanks to Theo, always, for your love and support. You make all of my challenges a little easier to overcome.

NOTES

NOTES

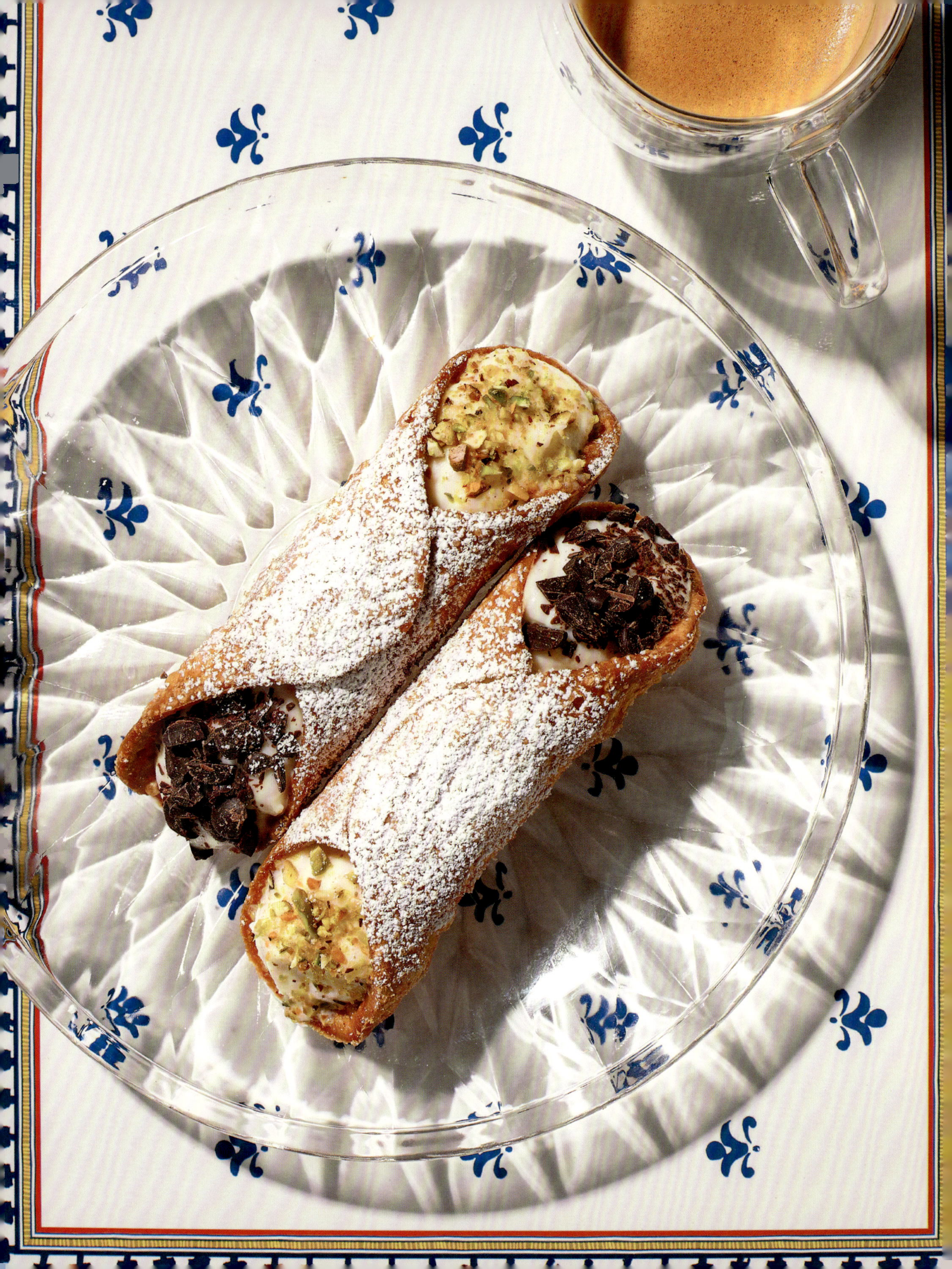

INDEX

A

Almonds
 Pasta con Pesto alla Trapanese, 73
 Pasta di Mandorla Cookies, 80
Anchovies
 Sfincione, 65
Arancini, 66–68
Avocados
 Fish Tacos, 38
 Poke Bowl, 31

B

Bananas
 Banana Pancakes (Roti Pisang), 126
 Tropical Sunrise Smoothie, 12
Basil
 Bruschetta, 61
 Pasta con Pesto alla Trapanese, 73
Bean sprouts
 Pad Thai Goong, 114
 "Rainbow" Rice Salad (Khao Yum), 118
Beef
 Loco Moco, 15
 Massaman Curry (Kaeng Massaman), 104
 Seared Steak with Shiitake Mushrooms and Miso Butter, 42
Biryani, Chicken (Khao Mok Gai), 110
Blood Orange and Fennel Salad, 56
Braciole Messinesi, 79
Bread and buns
 Brioche con Tuppo, 52
 Bruschetta, 61
 Coconut French Toast, 16
 Manapua, 25–26
 Roti, 99
 Sfincione, 65
Brioche col Tuppo, 52
Bruschetta, 61
Brussels sprouts
 Macadamia-Crusted Pork, 37
Butter Mochi, Ube-Marbled, 49

C

Cabbage
 Lime Pork (Moo Manao), 113
 "Rainbow" Rice Salad (Khao Yum), 118
Cakes
 Cassata, 91
 Coconut Cake, 46
Cannoli, 83
Caponata, 62
Carrots
 Poke Bowl, 31
 "Rainbow" Rice Salad (Khao Yum), 118
Cassata, 91
Cheese
 Arancini, 66–68
 Braciole Messinesi, 79
 Cannoli, 83
 Cassata, 91
 Ricotta Soufflé Pancakes, 17
 Sfincione, 65
 Warm Ricotta with Lemon and Olive Oil, 59
Chicken
 Chicken Biryani (Khao Mok Gai), 110
 Huli Huli Chicken, 35
 Tom Kha Gai, 117
 Yellow Curry (Kaeng Kari), 109
Chocolate
 Cannoli, 83
 Cassata, 91
 Pignolata, 88
Chowder, Coconut Seafood, 32
Coconut
 Coconut Cake, 46
 Coconut French Toast, 16
 Coconut Seafood Chowder, 32
 Macadamia Haupia Tart, 45
 "Rainbow" Rice Salad (Khao Yum), 118
 Sticky Rice and Mango, 129
 Ube-Marbled Butter Mochi, 49
Coffee Granita, 55
Cookies, Pasta di Mandorla, 80
Crab Fried Rice (Khao Phat Poo), 121

Cucumbers
 Lime Pork (Moo Manao), 113
 Poke Bowl, 31
 "Rainbow" Rice Salad (Khao Yum), 118
Curries
 Massaman Curry (Kaeng Massaman), 104
 Sour Curry (Kaeng Som), 100
 Yellow Curry (Kaeng Kari), 109

D

Desserts
 Banana Pancakes (Roti Pisang), 126
 Cannoli, 83
 Cassata, 91
 Coconut Cake, 46
 Coffee Granita, 55
 Gelato di Pistacchio, 84
 Lemon Prosecco Granita, 87
 Macadamia Haupia Tart, 45
 Pasta di Mandorla Cookies, 80
 Pignolata, 88
 Sticky Rice and Mango, 129
 Ube-Marbled Butter Mochi, 49
Drinks
 Thai Iced Tea, 125
 Tropical Sunrise Smoothie, 12

E

Edamame
 Poke Bowl, 31
 Seared Sesame-Crusted Mahi Mahi, 36
Eggplant
 Caponata, 62
 Pasta alla Norma, 74
Eggs
 Crab Fried Rice (Khao Phat Poo), 121
 Loco Moco, 15
 Pad Thai Goong, 114
 Rice Soup (Khao Tom Goong), 94
 Saimin, 41
 Thai-Style Omelet (Khao Khai Chiao), 97

F

Fennel
    Blood Orange and Fennel Salad, 56
    Pasta con le Sarde, 76

Fish
    Coconut Seafood Chowder, 32
    Fish Tacos, 38
    Lomi Lomi Salmon, 22
    Pasta con le Sarde, 76
    Poke Bowl, 31
    Saimin, 41
    Seared Sesame-Crusted Mahi Mahi, 36
    Sfincione, 65
    Sour Curry (Kaeng Som), 100

French Toast, Coconut, 16

Fritters. See Panelle

Fruit. *See specific fruits*

G

Garlic
    Bruschetta, 61
    Garlic Shrimp, 28

Gelato di Pistacchio, 84

Granita
    Coffee Granita, 55
    Lemon Prosecco Granita, 87

H

Haupia Macadamia Tart, 45
Huli Huli Chicken, 35

I

Iced Tea, Thai, 125

K

Kamaboko
    Saimin, 41

L

Lemon
    Lemon Prosecco Granita, 87
    Pignolata, 88
    Warm Ricotta with Lemon and Olive Oil, 59

Lime Pork (Moo Manao), 113
Lobster
    Coconut Seafood Chowder, 32
    Pasta Pescatore, 69
Loco Moco, 15
Lomi Lomi Salmon, 22

M

Macadamia-Crusted Pork, 37
Macadamia Haupia Tart, 45
Mahi mahi
    Fish Tacos, 38
    Seared Sesame-Crusted Mahi Mahi, 36
Malasadas, 18
Manapua, 25–26
Mango
    "Rainbow" Rice Salad (Khao Yum), 118
    Sticky Rice and Mango, 129
    Tropical Sunrise Smoothie, 12
Massaman Curry (Kaeng Massaman), 104
Miso Butter and Shiitake Mushrooms, Seared Steak with, 42
Mochi, Butter, Ube-Marbled, 49
Mushrooms
    Loco Moco, 15
    Seared Steak with Shiitake Mushrooms and Miso Butter, 42
    Tom Kha Gai, 117
    Tom Yum Goong, 103
Musubi, Spam, 21

N

Nam Prik Goong Siap, 108
Noodles
    Pad Thai Goong, 114
    Saimin, 41
Nori
    Spam Musubi, 21

O

Omelet, Thai-Style (Khao Khai Chiao), 97

P

Pad Thai Goong, 114
Pancakes
    Banana Pancakes (Roti Pisang), 126
    Ricotta Soufflé Pancakes, 17
Panelle, 70
Pasta. *See also* Noodles
    Pasta alla Norma, 74
    Pasta con le Sarde, 76
    Pasta con Pesto alla Trapanese, 73
    Pasta Pescatore, 69
Pastries
    Banana Pancakes (Roti Pisang), 126
    Cannoli, 83
    Pignolata, 88
Peanuts
    Massaman Curry (Kaeng Massaman), 104
    Pad Thai Goong, 114
    Satay, 107
Peppers and chiles
    Caponata, 62
    Huli Huli Chicken, 35
    Nam Prik Goong Siap, 108
    Sour Curry (Kaeng Som), 100
    Tom Yum Goong, 103
    Yellow Curry (Kaeng Kari), 109
Pignolata, 88
Pineapple
    Coconut Cake, 46
    Fish Tacos, 38
    Huli Huli Chicken, 35
    Poke Bowl, 31
    Tropical Sunrise Smoothie, 12
Pine nuts
    Caponata, 62
    Pasta con le Sarde, 76
Pistachios
    Blood Orange and Fennel Salad, 56
    Cannoli, 83
    Gelato di Pistacchio, 84
Pizza. See Sfincione
Poke Bowl, 31

Pork
    Braciole Messinesi, 79
    Crispy Pork (Moo Krop), 122
    Lime Pork (Moo Manao), 113
    Macadamia-Crusted Pork, 37
    Manapua, 25–26
    Rice Porridge (Jok), 96
    Saimin, 41
    Satay, 107
Potatoes
    Coconut Seafood Chowder, 32
    Macadamia-Crusted Pork, 37
    Massaman Curry
        (Kaeng Massaman), 104
    Yellow Curry (Kaeng Kari), 109
Prosciutto
    Braciole Messinesi, 79
Prosecco Lemon Granita, 87

R

"Rainbow" Rice Salad (Khao Yum), 118
Raisins
    Pasta con le Sarde, 76
Rice
    Arancini, 66–68
    Chicken Biryani
        (Khao Mok Gai), 110
    Crab Fried Rice
        (Khao Phat Poo), 121
    Crispy Pork (Moo Krop), 122
    Garlic Shrimp, 28
    Loco Moco, 15
    Poke Bowl, 31
    "Rainbow" Rice Salad
        (Khao Yum), 118
    Rice Porridge (Jok), 96
    Rice Soup (Khao Tom Goong), 94
    Spam Musubi, 21
    Sticky Rice and Mango, 129
    Thai-Style Omelet
        (Khao Khai Chiao), 97
Roti, 99
Rum
    Cassata, 91
    Pignolata, 88

S

Saimin, 41
Salads
    Blood Orange and Fennel Salad, 56
    "Rainbow" Rice Salad
        (Khao Yum), 118
Salmon, Lomi Lomi, 22
Sardines
    Pasta con le Sarde, 76
Satay, 107
Scallops
    Coconut Seafood Chowder, 32
    Pasta Pescatore, 69
Sesame-Crusted Mahi Mahi, Seared, 36
Sfincione, 65
Shellfish
    Coconut Seafood Chowder, 32
    Crab Fried Rice (Khao Phat Poo), 121
    Garlic Shrimp, 28
    Nam Prik Goong Siap, 108
    Pad Thai Goong, 114
    Pasta Pescatore, 69
    Rice Soup (Khao Tom Goong), 94
    Sour Curry (Kaeng Som), 100
    Tom Yum Goong, 103
Shrimp and prawns
    Coconut Seafood Chowder, 32
    Garlic Shrimp, 28
    Nam Prik Goong Siap, 108
    Pad Thai Goong, 114
    Pasta Pescatore, 69
    Rice Soup (Khao Tom Goong), 94
    Sour Curry (Kaeng Som), 100
    Tom Yum Goong, 103
Smoothie, Tropical Sunrise, 12
Soups
    Coconut Seafood Chowder, 32
    Rice Porridge (Jok), 96
    Rice Soup (Khao Tom Goong), 94
    Saimin, 41
    Tom Kha Gai, 117
    Tom Yum Goong, 103
Sour Curry (Kaeng Som), 100
Spam Musubi, 21

T

Tacos, Fish, 38
Tart, Macadamia Haupia, 45
Tea, Thai Iced, 125
Tofu
    Pad Thai Goong, 114
Tomatoes
    Arancini, 66–68
    Bruschetta, 61
    Caponata, 62
    Fish Tacos, 38
    Lomi Lomi Salmon, 22
    Pasta alla Norma, 74
    Pasta con Pesto alla Trapanese, 73
    Pasta Pescatore, 69
    Sfincione, 65
Tom Kha Gai, 117
Tom Yum Goong, 103
Tuna
    Poke Bowl, 31

U

Ube-Marbled Butter Mochi, 49

V

Vegetables. *See also specific vegetables*
    Nam Prik Goong Siap, 108

Y

Yellow Curry (Kaeng Kari), 109

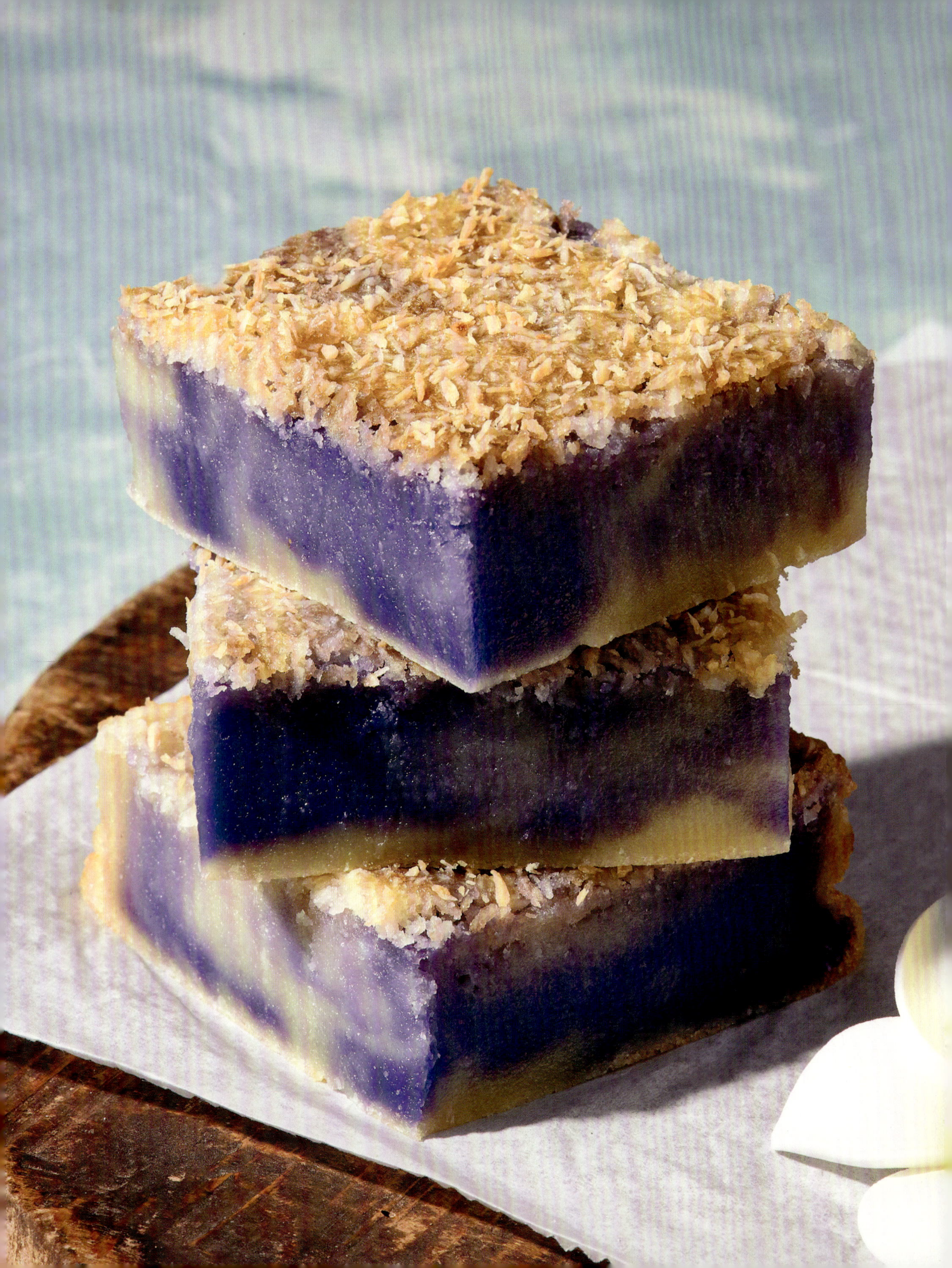

Insight Editions
P.O. Box 3088
San Rafael, CA 94912
insighteditions.com

Find us on Facebook: www.facebook.com/InsightEditions
Follow us on Instagram: @insighteditions

Copyright © 2025 Warner Bros. Entertainment Inc.
THE WHITE LOTUS and all related characters and elements © & ™ Home Box Office, Inc. (s25)

All rights reserved. Published by Insight Editions, San Rafael, California, in 2025.

No part of this book may be reproduced in any form without written permission from the publisher.

ISBN: 979-8-88663-881-3

Publisher: Raoul Goff
SVP, Group Publisher: Vanessa Lopez
VP, Creative: Chrissy Kwasnik
VP, Manufacturing: Alix Nicholaeff
Editorial Director: Thom O'Hearn
Art Director: Stuart Smith
Senior Designer: Judy Wiatrek Trum
Editor: Alexis Sattler
Assistant Editor: Sami Alvarado
Managing Editor: Shannon Ballesteros
Production Manager: Deena Hashem
Strategic Production Planner: Lina s Palma-Temena

Photographer: Carla Choy
Food Stylist: Alexander Roberts
Associate Food Stylist: Joey Firoben
Assistant Food Stylist: Emily Cooper

ROOTS of PEACE   REPLANTED PAPER

Insight Editions, in association with Roots of Peace, will plant two trees for each tree used in the manufacturing of this book. Roots of Peace is an internationally renowned humanitarian organization dedicated to eradicating land mines worldwide and converting war-torn lands into productive farms and wildlife habitats. Roots of Peace will plant two million fruit and nut trees in Afghanistan and provide farmers there with the skills and support necessary for sustainable land use.

Manufactured in China by Insight Editions

10 9 8 7 6 5 4 3 2 1

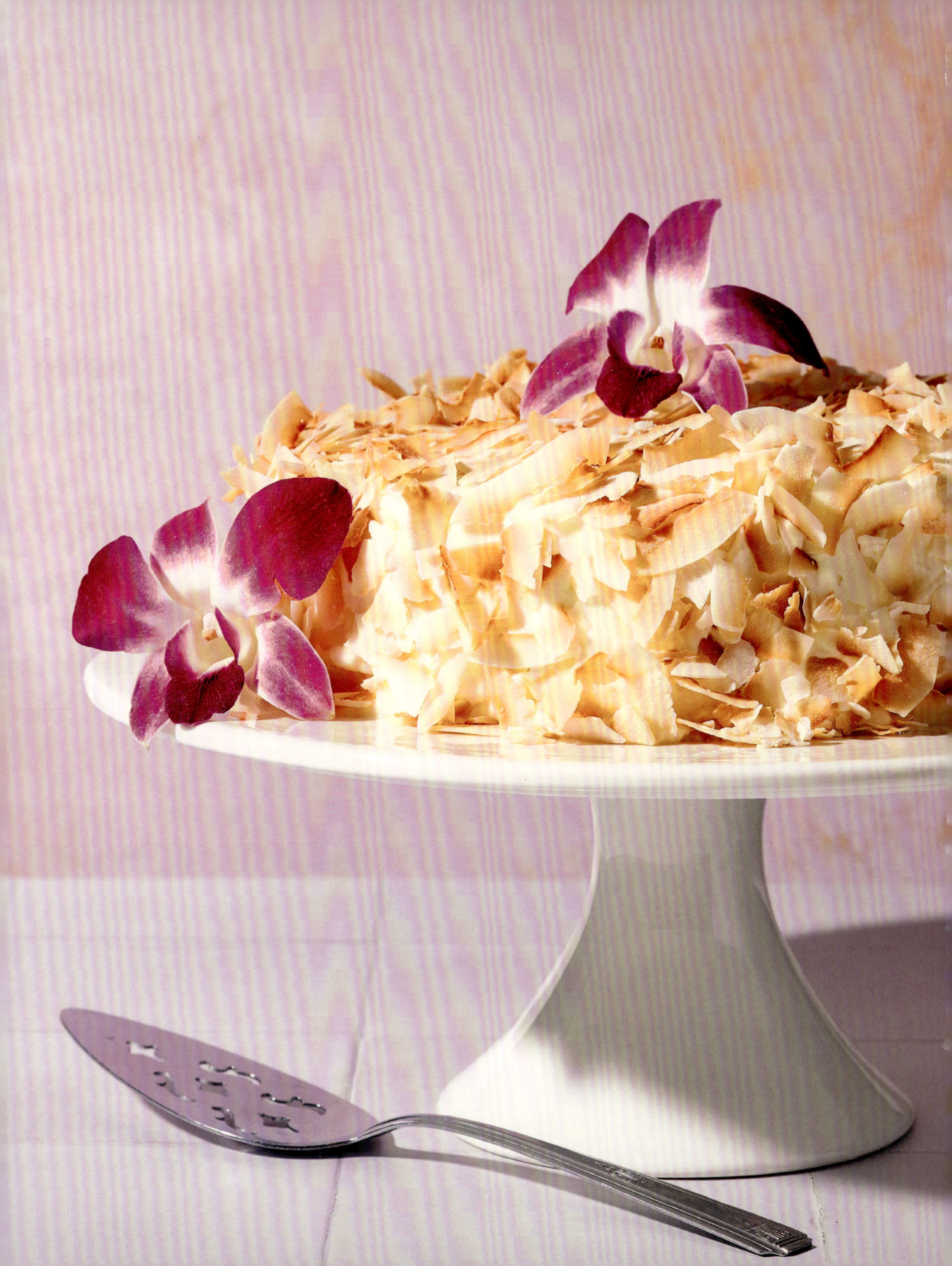